THE ICE EXPERIENCE

JEFF LOWE

D0111869

Produced by Book Developers, Inc.
of Chicago, Illinois,
for Contemporary Books, Inc.

Contemporary Books, Inc.
Chicago

Library of Congress Cataloging in Publication Data
Lowe, Jeff
    The ice experience

    Includes index.
    1. 1. Snow and ice climbing.   2. Snow and ice
climbing—United States.   3. Snow and ice
climbing—Canada.   I. Title.
GV200.3.L68   1979   796.9   78-23456
ISBN 0-8092-7512-0
ISBN 0-8092-7511-2 pbk.

For

Ralph, Elgene, and Christie

Published by Contemporary Books, Inc.
180 North Michigan Avenue, Chicago, Illinois 60601
Manufactured in the United States of America
Library of Congress Catalog Card Number: 78-23456
International Standard Book Number: 0-8092-7512-0 (cloth)
                                    0-8092-7511-2 (paper)

Published simultaneously in Canada by
Beaverbooks
953 Dillingham Road
Pickering, Ontario L1W 1Z7
Canada

Contents

vii Acknowledgments

ix Introduction

Chapter 1 *1* Icy Roots, Crystal Blossoms

Chapter 2 *43* The Hazards and the Gear

Chapter 3 *66* Regimen for Snow Sloggers and Ice Dancers

Chapter 4 *120* The Hardwater Guide

Chapter 5 *175* One Man's Frostbite

205 Index

Acknowledgments

I would like to thank the following people:

Greg Lowe for his excellent conversions of color slides to black-and-white prints;

John Ruger for taking the technique photographs;

Jeff Long and **Pat Ament** for their constructive criticism of my writing style (or lack of same);

Mike Kennedy, Mike Lowe, Mike Weis, Christie Northrop, Bill Roos, and many others for reading parts of the manuscript;

John Roskelley, John Evans, Peter Breu, Wes Kraus, Jim Knight, Mike Kennedy, Ken Cook, Pat Callis, Bob Dodds, Christie Northrop, Mike Lowe, Greg Lowe, and **George Lowe** for permission to use their photos; and

Sherry Livingston for typing and preparing the manuscript.

Without these people this book never could have been completed.

Introduction

Say the words "mountain climber" to the proverbial man-on-the-street and what image have you conjured? Likely, a vision of sheer rock walls with people clinging precariously to them. There's another type of mountain, however, that offers equal opportunity for adventure. Although it might be only a vague shimmering in the minds' eyes of many, the "ice mountain" is not a fiction. It has been there all along, although the peak often was hidden in clouds of disinterest. Until recently, only a few individuals were attracted to ice; perhaps by the magnetism of its mystery.

Now, the fine and little-known sport of ice climbing is experiencing a boom in North America. The small group that once virtually "owned" the ice-covered mountains must now rise early, contrary to all the old customs, to be first on the icefall.

And now one of the old and nearly illiterate climbers has come down to replace his axe (temporarily) with pen and face a new sort of challenge. It is inevitable, of course; where there is so much interest there will soon be ink.

There is one main difference between rock and ice climbing. The quality of rock runs the whole spectrum from crumbling sandstone to iron-hard granite, but given pieces do not change a great deal from week to week or even from year to year. Ice, on the other hand, exhibits daily, even hourly, changes. A ribbon of hardened water might exist only in the morning hours after a hard freeze; by late afternoon, the only remains will be a wet streak on the rock. The ice climber, besides attaining a degree of technical proficiency, must develop a "feel" for these ever-changing conditions.

The two branches of mountaineering have similarities, most of which concern the attitudes one assumes when approaching a climb. The rock climber, if he or she so chooses, might reject all tools—even shoes and clothing—to achieve a totally "pure" experience. However, one is obliged to use tools to climb ice. This is not a justification for indiscriminate use of

The ice climber, besides attaining technical proficiency, must develop a "feel" for ever-changing conditions. (Photo by John Roskelley)

technology. The purity of the ice experience lies in learning to use the minimum number of aids in the most efficient manner possible. The first climb of Canada's Takkakkaw Falls took six days, the climbers ascending by means of aid slings clipped to their ice axes and returning to base camp each night with the help of a long series of ropes fixed to their high point. But the second ascent was accomplished in *seven hours* by others who had pared their tools and attitudes to the essentials.

The differences between the two media stand out at first glance: the naked rock climber and the bundled and spiked ice climber. And although the bare-handed communication with rock is direct, the sensitive person can develop an equal rapport with ice through his or her hardware, and the two types of climbing ultimately offer the same rewards and satisfactions.

Ice climbing is one part of the entire sport of mountaineering, but that part must be divided further for a clear understanding of the modern scene. The traditional terrain for ice

The "purity" of the ice experience lies in using the minimum number of aids in the most efficient manner possible. (Photo by Jeff Lowe)

climbing is found only in the high mountains—on glaciers, icefields, and couloirs. The ice types of these features vary widely, but all have one thing in common: the ice began as some form of frozen precipitation, and through the influences of such things as time, pressure, and heat, it changed into something identified generically as *Alpine ice*.

In recent years, a "new" kind of ice has grabbed the spotlight. *Water ice* can be found wherever water and freezing temperatures coincide. It is generally much more brittle than its Alpine cousin and often much steeper. The difficulties of

Alpine ice—whether found in the high mountains, on glaciers or icefields, or in couloirs—begins as frozen precipitation and develops through the influences of time, pressure, and heat. (Photo by Jeff Lowe)

frozen waterfalls, for instance, are enough to challenge today's climber who, with greatly improved gear and without the psychological burden of the unknown, makes light of all but a few of the hardest Alpine climbs.

Alpine ice climbing developed slower in North America than it did in the European Alps. In 1938 Anderl Heckmair and Ludwig Vorg front-pointed the icefields during the first ascent of the North Face of the Eiger in Switzerland while as late as 1965 a respected local spokesman considered two climbers foolhardy for doing the same thing in Wyoming's Black Ice Couloir.

With ascents of The Weeping Wall, Bourgeau Left-Hand, The Black Dike, Repentance, Green Gully, Bridalveil, and Mahlen's Peak Waterfall in the early 1970s, North Americans were the first to climb extensively on frozen waterfalls. They discovered a totally different sort of climbing from that which had been so thoroughly equipped, choreographed, and cataloged by the Germans, French, and Scots.

This book is a kind of celebration of the "slippery game" as it has evolved and is played on this continent. Throughout, the reader will be aware of the author's personal bias. I make no excuse for that. The beauty of the ice experience lies not in faceless absolutes but rather in the personal approach of each individual.

One final note: newcomers to the basic methods of ascent should seek competent instruction from an experienced friend or professional before attempting to use the techniques discussed in Chapter 3. In making the transition to ice, even climbers thoroughly familiar with rock techniques often discover a pitfall or two. Chapter 3 was written with a certain amount of technical knowledge assumed.

1

Icy Roots, Crystal Blossoms

As a young climber—barely a teenager really—I hung out each summer in the Tetons, either at the old Climber's Camp south of Jenny Lake or around the Exum Guide's Camp, where I was either tolerated or overlooked. (I'm not certain which). Although I was too young to take part in the good times or tall tales at the famous Teton Tea Parties, I managed to be near those climbers who had traveled to other areas in the United States and Canada, and I'd catch the drift of the latest happenings in Yosemite, Alaska, the Bugaboos, and elsewhere.

Most of the talk was about rock climbing. The summer after the North American Wall on Yosemite's El Capitan was climbed, I caught several conversations around the campfires and picnic tables. The sentiment seemed to be unanimous: Pratt, Robbins, Chouinard, and Frost had made the hardest rock climb in the world! I was in awe of such talk from the vanguard of the rock scene but not as much as when some bearded, world-wise climber would talk about the Black Ice Couloir or the Willis Wall.

Even the bearded ones spoke of these ice climbs with slight trembles in their voices. In North America at that time the dangers of ice were greatly exaggerated in climbers' minds. Only about a dozen persons on the whole continent could be called competent ice climbers by European standards. The rest of the climbing community was "psyched out." I was among that group, cowering at the very *thought* of the harsh world to be found on the cold side of the mountain. Rockfalls . . . storms . . . avalanches . . . no protection—the worst!

Since that time, of course, the situation has changed. To begin with, a few climbers who had "done it all" on rock started looking to the high mountains for fresh challenges. While looking, they could hardly fail to see the ice and snow that always accompanies great altitude. Those who journeyed to the Alps began to see that here, indeed, was a fine medium for adventurous climbing. Not an unreasonable challenge either, the way the Europeans were doing it.

By the late 1960s and early 1970s ice climbing had come of age. On this side of the Atlantic, the climbs being done equaled the hard Alpine routes, and a new type of ice climbing was developing a substantial following—winter climbing on ice-covered crags and frozen waterfalls. Today, climbers experienced in this sort of activity can travel to all parts of the world and accomplish the most difficult ice climbs. That's quite a turnaround in less than twenty years!

How did this come about? The following account, short though it is, might help to explain the sudden popularity of ice climbing. Separating the story of ice climbing in North America from that of rock climbing and general mountaineering is difficult. And, unfortunately, I do not have the space in this book for a comprehensive review. Those interested in a complete history should read Chris Jones's fine volume, *Climbing in North America*, published by the American Alpine Club in 1976.

A GLANCE AT THE OLD DAYS

Before we talk about the modern evolution of ice climbing, it's a good idea to review the years prior to the early 1960s to establish a backdrop for later developments. Also, even though it is my premise that North America was only a stagnant backwater in terms of ice climbing, there were certain climbers who apparently didn't know that. Over the years, they established a small number of excellent ice climbs, and those climbs deserve to be recorded.

In 1786 Jacques Balmat and Dr. Michel Paccard were the first men ever to stand on the summit of Europe: France's 15,771-foot Mont Blanc. This marks the beginning of Alpine mountaineering. Search as we might, however, we cannot find a similar date to denote so decisively the origin of the sport in North America. Some say Scottish botanist David Douglas was the first real mountaineer on this continent, basing the claim on an entry in his journal during an 1827 trip through the Canadian Rockies. In the journal Douglas tells of climbing an icy peak above Athabasca Pass simply because he was "desirous" of doing so. Others suggest that the ascent of Mount Rainier by Hazard Stevens and Philemon Von Trump in 1870, during which they employed both a rope and ice axes, should be taken as the true birth of the sport in the New World. Yet another writer has chosen the year 1888 as the beginning of real climbing in this land, with the ascent of Mount Bonney in the Selkirk Range of Canada by the English clergymen Green and Swanzy. There probably will never be agreement on an exact date, but what does it really matter? By the late 1800s the sport of mountain climbing had found a toehold on this continent.

The early climbers did not seem to differentiate between rock and ice, the two media of ascent. Whatever offered the easiest approach to a certain peak was the key, be it pure ice, pure rock, or a mixture of each. Reaching the summit was the goal, to be able to "look down upon the rest of the world." Quite naturally, then, the climbers of the dry Sierra Nevadas

The Kain Face of Mount Robson. Conrad Kain made the first ascent of the peak via the Northeast Face and upper Southeast Ridge in 1913. (Photo by Jeff Lowe)

or Colorado Rockies were destined to develop rock-climbing skills to the virtual exclusion of snow and ice techniques. Just the opposite was true in the snowy mountains of the Pacific Northwest and Canada. The Canadian Rockies, in fact, were the scene of the first truly extended and difficult ice climb: the first ascent of Mount Robson, via the Northeast Face and upper Southeast Ridge, on July 31, 1913. The protagonist of this climb was not a Canadian or an American but a young Austrian mountain guide named Conrad Kain.

The First Ascent of Mount Robson

The most accomplished ringmaster could not have arranged a better set of opponents. Kain was the greatest climber of the day, and Mount Robson, at 12,972 feet the highest and most imposing summit of the Canadian Rockies, was still unclimbed after a number of determined efforts.

The Shushwap Indians called Robson *Yuh-hai-has-kun*, "the mountain of the spiral road"—an apt name for the southern view of the stratified ramparts that rise almost ten thousand feet above Kinney Lake. Kain did not choose to approach from that side, however, but from the northeast, where, as his contemporary James Outram said, "Enormous seas of ice sweep from the Alpine heights."

The day before the climb of Mount Robson, Kain and his two partners in the venture, an American, A. H. MacCarthy, and a Canadian, W. W. Foster, made a training climb on nearby Mount Resplendent. From a 10,000-foot camp at the head of the Robson Glacier between the two peaks, they had a fine day on the West Ridge to Resplendent, the sun glittering beautifully off the snow and ice that crunched under their

North side of Mount Robson. North Ridge is on left; North Face is in center. (Photo by Greg Lowe)

nailed boots. On Robson, Kain would pay for the good luck of the weather with the pain and impaired vision of partial snow blindness. But he was not the sort to let a "small thing" like that stop him from making the climb.

By 10:00 A.M. on July 31 the trio was already halfway up the initial 1,000-foot face of snow and ice, with Kain in the lead, chopping with his long axe. A hemp rope dangled uselessly down from Kain's waist to those of his partners. (Actually, in this instance the rope was worse than useless since the climbers had no ice screws or pitons with which to belay. If one man would have slipped, they all would have tumbled into a heap on the glacier below.) Kain carved deep steps that

Looking down past Dan Davis during the first ascent of the North Face of Mount Robson in 1963. Circle indicates basecamp. (Photo by Pat Callis)

tilted slightly inward, toward the mountain, providing good support for nailed boots. Soon they passed the objective dangers of the face—the threatening ice cliff and the avalanches that would begin in early afternoon—and began the final leg of the climb through the steps of ice and snow that comprise the upper East Ridge.

The ridge was not as easy as its general angle had led Kain to hope. It rose in a series of steps and terraces. While the terraces were relatively flat, the steps were quite steep and often composed of hard ice. Kain's arms grew weary from chopping, the ice chips rattled down onto MacCarthy and Foster, who were shivering at the belay, and time was lost in the intensity of the efforts. Then, almost without warning, Kain found himself on the highest mushroom of windblown ice; nearly two miles of air yawned beneath his feet. In every direction the land was a jumble of white-capped mountains. The sight of Mount Whitehorn's elegant pyramid to the west brought two-year-old memories of climbing alone to its apex. Deep-forested valleys gemmed with silt-blue lakes and ribboned with metallic rivers entertained his downward gaze. Who knows what he felt? The moment was his alone.

When Foster and MacCarthy arrived at Kain's side, he greeted them simply: "Gentlemen, that's as far as I can take you."

With the example that Kain and company provided on the ice of Mount Robson, you might reasonably expect that a rich tradition of North American ice climbing, analogous to developments in the Alps, would follow. However, it did not happen. Why? Part of the answer might be that there were relatively few active climbers in North America during the early twentieth century. The numerous opportunities for making first ascents completely on rock—especially in the western portion of the continent—relieved climbers of the burden of mastering snow and ice as well. The Kain Face (as it is called now) was climbed in 1913 only because this route seemed the easiest and most practical way to reach the summit of Mount Robson. The ascent of *Yuh-hai-has-kun* was a tour de force of climbing and was years ahead of its time. We must investigate elsewhere to discover when and where climbers began seeking out the "ice experience" for its own sake.

Pinnacle Gully

In the relatively low altitudes of New England mountains, winter conditions can be amazingly severe. Subzero temperatures seem colder there than in the Rocky Mountains because of much higher humidity. Water ice tends to drape itself over nearly every available precipice. Today, these frozen waterfalls and ice smears on the rock are commonly dotted with rope teams from the first moment they become climbable in December until March or early April thaws.

This popularity is recent, however. When members of the Harvard and Yale mountaineering clubs first investigated the ice-filled gullies of Huntington Ravine in the late 1920s, they were quite alone. Huntington Ravine is located at an elevation of about 5,000 feet on the eastern side of New Hampshire's Mount Washington. In summer the ravine's gullies are little more than vegetated streambeds and rockfall paths. But under full winter ice and snow, it appeared to Noel O'Dell that these same gullies might provide good winter practice for summer climbing in the Alps, just as the winter hills of Scotland were used as a training ground by his fellow Englishmen. More than that, O'Dell thought that the gullies might provide good sport in their own right. In 1928 he and several others climbed the easiest of the gullies. With this climb as a precedent, other climbers from the university clubs took up the challenge and headed for the avalanche-prone ravine and its 1,000- to 1,500-foot ice and snow climbs, the finest of which is Pinnacle Gully.

The winter following the ascent of O'Dell's Gully, at least two attempts were made on Pinnacle, one by the team of Robert Underhill and Lincoln O'Brien, two of the strongest rock climbers of the day. The previous summer they had accomplished the first climb of the 1,000 feet of granite on

Cannon Cliff. Their attempt on Pinnacle was thwarted, however, by the brittle ice on a 60-degree bulge near the top of the first pitch.

Pinnacle Gully was climbed eventually in the winter of 1930. Using the standard technique of the time (which has been described as the "two-handed stand and hew"), Julian Whittlesey and his partner, Scoville, climbed the five pitches, which are angled, on average, at about 50 degrees, in less than 6 hours. This was very good time, as Pinnacle's 600 feet of brittle water ice has seen several later ascents that required more than 10 hours.

The important thing about these early New England winter ice climbs is not their difficulty, for they are no longer considered hard, but the attitude of those who made the climbs. Here were people who did not have to climb ice in order to reach a summit. The gullies in Huntington Ravine don't even go to the top of the mountain. On the contrary, O'Dell, Whittlesey, Scoville, and their friends purposely sought out the ice and found it in one of the least hospitable environments around.

Ice climbing for its own sake had begun in North America, and its few devotees joined the larger ranks of Germans, Austrians, French, English, Scots, and Italians who had discovered in the Alps and in Scotland that ice can be as rewarding to climb as rock. But although the popularity of ice climbing in Europe continued to grow, techniques continued to evolve, and the hardest and biggest faces were climbed, ice climbing on this side of the Atlantic remained the passion of only a few. The next advance would once again be inspired by a European climber.

The North Ridge of Mount Robson

Certain mountains have exerted more than their share of influence on the development of ice climbing. Glacier-draped Mount Rainier has provided almost one hundred years worth of "last great problems" for climbers in the Northwest. Mount

McKinley, the highest peak on the continent, whose Indian name is *Denali*, also has provided generation after generation with new challenges, from the amazing "Sourdough Climb" in 1913 (when three miners climbed the 8,000 vertical feet from their 11,000-foot base camp to the summit of the North Peak and back in one day!) to the British Direct on the 10,000-foot South Face in 1976. Robson, too, has been such a mountain from the first ascent (of which we've already spoken) to the 1963 climb of the 55-degree ice slope on the North Face. After the ascent of Pinnacle Gully in 1930, the North Ridge of Robson represented the next advance in ice-climbing standards—one that would last a long time.

It was the summer of 1938. In Switzerland the Eigerwand was climbed for the first time. In Canada it seemed to Fuhrer, Hainsworth, and Carlson that the North Ridge of Robson, which rose steep and icy for more than 2,000 feet above their camp on the Helmet Col, would be hard enough. To the left was the smaller lobe of ice that had been climbed by Kain and his party 25 years earlier but which now seemed a bit commonplace to this group of experienced climbers.

The sun was just peaking above Mount Resplendent to the east when the three crossed the bergschrund onto the base of the ridge. Fuhrer, a Swiss guide, was in the lead. Once again an Alpine guide was setting ice-climbing standards on this continent, supported by adventurous locals.

As Fuhrer chopped his way up an ice-filled couloir that sliced through the layered rocks of the ridge, he used the same technique as his predecessor, Kain, except for crampons, which had taken the place of nailed boots, and rock and ice pitons, which he occasionally placed for safety. Fuhrer was unaware that on the Eiger, Heckmair and Vorg were front-pointing the icefields. Twelve hours after starting, the small band of explorers dragged themselves one by one over the summit cornice, feeling that sense of accomplishment that only the climber of a difficult new route can know.

The North Ridge of Mount Robson is not as great a challenge as the face of the Eiger, which epitomized the state of the art in the Alps at that time, but it remained the finest climb of its kind in North America for many years. Shortly after the ridge was climbed, World War II virtually halted the progress of ice climbing. When the war ended and climbing picked up again, interest seemed to be directed almost entirely toward rock, except by climbers of the Northwest, especially Fred Beckey and his friends.

Mount Deborah

Until quite recently almost all of the big Alaskan mountains were climbed in "expedition style." That is, permanent camps, carefully stocked with food and gear, were established along the route, and on technically difficult routes fixed ropes were used so that climbers would have a quick path of retreat in the event of storm, injury, and so forth. There is nothing intrinsically wrong with these methods, and they have supported a large number of high-quality efforts. But a good argument can be made that expedition-style climbs have failed over the years to account for a single advance in standards or commitment.

It is only necessary to recall the Sourdoughs on *Denali*, three tough miners who climbed in one day a route that has required weeks by subsequent expedition parties. The problem with expedition-style climbing is that it requires a slow, tedious build-up that is almost *bound* to eliminate the possibility of a spontaneous and inspired ascent. Instead, the climber comes to resemble a cog in a machine that operates in quasi-militaristic fashion.

In 1954 an Alaskan climb was made that set a standard for boldness that would not be equaled for years to come. Fred Beckey, a German climber by the name of Henry Meybohm, and Heinrich Harrer, an Austrian who had participated in the first ascent of the North Face of the Eiger, climbed 12,339-foot Mount Deborah. They moved "Alpine style," that is, without fixing ropes and moving their high camp up with them as they progressed.

From the start of the climb at about 7,000 feet on the Yanert Glacier to the summit of the mountain took only three days. The final day consisted of a climb up the steep western slopes to the notch between the middle peak and the main summit and from there to the top by way of a badly corniced ridge. Twenty-one years later, on the occasion of the second ascent of the mountain (which required thirty-six days!), Brian Okonek described his first up-close view of this summit ridge as follows: "When I first peeked over the middle summit and saw the full sweep of the summit ridge, fantastic wind sculptures of wild-looking cornices met my eyes. . . . Incredible! Unreal!"

The first climb of Deborah was as far advanced for its day as the Kain Face of Robson had been in 1913. Yet even today some climbers are still using expedition tactics on easier mountains. Beckey, Meybohm, and Harrer definitely had pushed back the horizon of the ice climber. And on that occasion, the local climber, Beckey, was not towed to the top by the Europeans—he was an equal partner in every way.

Though Deborah was the most advanced ice climb of its time, a few other climbers actively sought the ice experience during the decade of the fifties, primarily in the Northwest on the volcanic peaks and on a few summits of the North Cascades, notably Mounts Shuksan, Maude, and Fury. Beckey was involved in many of these climbs, partnered by people such as Bob Craig and Don Gordon.

There was another group of climbers, too, from the Ellensburg and Yakima, Washington, areas who, acting independently of the Seattle-based climbers, made many good ice climbs, such as the second ascents of both the Ptarmigan and Liberty Ridges and the first ascent of the Curtis Ridge, all of which are good ice climbs on the north side of 14,410-foot Mount Rainier. Dave Mahre (who took part in all of these climbs) and his friends had taken it upon themselves to learn the technique of front-pointing, and they made use of it during these ascents. Contemporary European methods finally were beginning to find their way across the Atlantic.

The stage was set for the sixties, a transition period after which Jim MacCarthy could with justification entitle an article written for the *American Alpine Journal* "Coming of Age—Ice Climbing in North America."

References

1 Becker, Bryan. "On a Winter's Day," *Climbing*, No. 45.
2 Cole and Wilcox. "Shades of Blue," *Eastern Mountain Sports*, 1976.
3 Jones, Chris. *Climbing in North America*. California: American Alpine Club.
4 Kain, Conrad. *Where the Clouds Can Go*. Charles T. Bradford Company, reprinted 1954.
5 Okonek, Brian. "Deborah," *American Alpine Journal*, 1976.
6 Outram, James. *In the Heart of the Canadian Rockies*. New York: Macmillan, 1906.
7 Rebuffat, Gatson. *The Mont Blanc Massif*. New York: Oxford University Press, 1975.

NORTH FACES AND CURVED PICKS: A DECADE OF DISCOVERY

The first ascent of Yosemite's Lost Arrow Chimney in 1947 was the beginning of big-wall rock climbing in North America. John Salathe and Anton Nelson spent five suffocatingly hot days on this 1,500-foot climb with very little food, water, or gear. It was a triumph of the spirit and a fine precedent for the following years of rock exploration.

The 1954 climb of Mount Deborah could have provided a similar stimulus for ice climbing, but it did not. Ice climbing seemed isolated from the mainstream of Alpine climbing, and consequently people were ignorant of the techniques and safeguards developed for the sport. The feeling of the time, with regard to ice, is illustrated by this quote from Orrin and Lorraine Bonney's *Field Guide to the Wind River Range*: "Black ice is [the] most difficult and dangerous of mountain faces and should be avoided when possible." If you couple

that ignorance and fear with the exaggerated safety conscious-
ness that ruled supreme in the main circles of North American
mountaineering, it's not hard to see why the sport on this
continent had become such a stunted child of its European
parent. By the early sixties the arm of rock climbing had
become strong enough to wield a heavy hammer for several
days, but the arm of ice climbing had atrophied through
disuse.

Into this overblown cloud of caution stepped Charlie Bell.

The Willis Wall, Mount Rainier

The Willis Wall rises 4,000 feet from the Carbon Glacier to
Liberty Cap, the northernmost summit of Mount Rainier. Its
most prominent feature is an ice cliff, 250 feet thick, that
spans the entire wall just below the top. This ice cliff, and the
rumbling avalanches of ice blocks it occasionally drops down
the wall, had prevented any serious attempt at climbing the
face. In the Alps similar ice walls had been climbed in the
thirties, but by American standards the risks had seem unjus-
tifiable. However, people such as Dave Mahre, whom we
already have met in connection with the north ridges of
Rainier, and Gene Prater had run out of climbs to challenge
them. Something new was required, and the Willis Wall was
it. In the summer of 1961 Prater, Mahre, and several others set
out for an attempt on the wall. In their support party, which
was required by Park Service regulations, was Charlie Bell, an
enigmatic figure of Northwest climbing.

The weather was bad for the attempt, and the climbers were
soon in full retreat—all except Charlie Bell. Steve Miller, a
member of the support party, recalls:

"Charlie, armed with a couple of pounds of Baby Ruths
and two or three tarps, settled down for a long sleep. Some
days later, he returned to Seattle, telling us that he had slept
for a day and a half until it stopped raining and climbed the
Willis Wall while it was good and frozen. It seemed strange,
but so did Charlie."

Charlie's veracity soon was under fire from the "guns" of Northwest climbing. After all, if they were so awed by the Willis Wall, which they considered the *ultimate* problem on Mount Rainier, how could Bell, who had not even been chosen for the assault party, simply wander up the Carbon Glacier and solo the route? Preposterous! Where was the evidence? They wanted proof, but there was only the man's word. They didn't believe him. And a terrible thing happens when climbers start calling for "proof" of another's ascent: the sport loses its dignity.

Charlie Bell actually did provide proof of his ascent in the form of photographs taken from high on the wall. But the pundits said they could have been taken from somewhere else—perhaps from the side of the Liberty Ridge, whicp borders the face on the right.

It wasn't until the second ascent of his route (Damocles' Rib) in the winter of 1970 that Charlie finally was vindicated. During their climb, Jim Wickwire and Alex Bertulis took photographs that later were compared to the ones Bell had taken. Several of the photos obviously were taken from the same place; certain features matched perfectly. Bell had not lied. On the contrary, he had made a breakthrough, not in terms of technical difficulty but in the more important realm of expanding the concept of human potential.

Another important climb was made in the summer of 1961. Ray Jaquot and Herb Swedlund climbed the gash on the West Face of the Grand Teton, which had become known as the Black Ice Couloir because of the dark color of the ice. Again the climb was not a technical breakthrough, as the climbers relied heavily on step cutting, but the 11 hours they spent in the gully were additional evidence to support the growing belief that this sort of climb was not prohibitively dangerous.

Other climbers sat up and began taking notes. Ice climbing still retained its mystery, but more climbers were feeling the desire to experience it. New techniques were experimented with, notably front-pointing with an ice axe in one hand and a "dagger," or ice piton, in the other. Ice screws also were introduced, which greatly increased the security of ice climbing.

Over the next several years other routes were accomplished on the Willis Wall (though Bell's was not repeated). The Black Ice Couloir was climbed again (this time with fewer cut steps), and Pat Callis and Dan Davis climbed the North Face of Mount Robson, a beautiful 2,000-foot sheet of ice and snow to the right of the 1938 North Ridge route. Good climbs all of these, but what would be the next real advance in technique or attitude?

The Hummingbird Ridge, Mount Logan

Jules Verne once said, "Anything one man can imagine, other men can make real." We're used to hearing such declarations of the ever-expanding quality of human potential. Perhaps it is true—or perhaps only a delusion of the species. But six men made a climb in 1965 that makes me feel that Jules Verne was right.

Mount Logan is located in the St. Elias Range, Yukon Territory, Canada. Its 19,850-foot central peak is the second highest point in North America, only 470 feet lower than the summit of Mount McKinley. It is a huge mountain, whose summit plateau comprises nearly 10 square miles and whose

The south side of Mount Logan with Hummingbird Ridge in center of photograph. (Photo by John Evans)

ridges span 24 miles in an east-west direction. Three south ridges drop 14,000 feet to the Seward Glacier. The Central Ridge consists of 6 miles of unbelievably contorted cornice, crag, and ice slope. It is so large that one-fifth of the ridge would be a major climb. To climb it in semi-Alpine style (i.e., fixing ropes between camps but not down to base) was an impossible dream in 1965. But that did not stop Al Steck, John Evans, Frank Coale, Jim Wilson, Paul Bacon, and Dick Long from doing it.

After three weeks of intense effort, during which the climbers wondered at the sanity of their actions ("This route is sheer madness"), they had not yet reached a "bump" on the Ridge at 13,000 feet, which they had designated the "Snow Dome." With less than half the ridge climbed and much more than half of their food consumed, most parties would have elected to retreat while that option was still open. But these climbers kept at it. Evans later described the ridge that they followed:

"A high wire in the sky, artistically daubed with a stiff

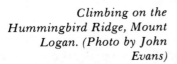

Climbing on the Hummingbird Ridge, Mount Logan. (Photo by John Evans)

meringue of snow; a bottomless fantasy of cornices and flut-
ings.''

Finally, on August 6, one month after starting out, they
reached the summit. "Weaker than we realized, we staggered
like drunks, . . . '' But they were six very happy and satisfied
drunks, for they had gone out on a limb, and, as Frank Scully
says, "isn't that where the fruit is?''

Early on in the climb, Steck had been ascending a couloir
on the side of the ridge. He heard a buzzing sound and
instinctively protected his head against what he thought was a
falling rock. But the buzzing continued; no rock could fall so
slowly. He looked in the direction of the sound only to see a
tiny hummingbird hovering and darting above his red pack.
The incongruity of the spectacle stayed in Steck's mind
throughout the climb—a source of wonder and comfort that
sustained him through the difficulties. The gigantic climb
eventually was named after the tiny creature.

The South Ridge of Logan was indeed a breakthrough. To
this day, no climb in North America has required a greater
level of commitment. But technically the Hummingbird Ridge
climb was of less importance. The only innovation used
extensively was a snow shovel instead of an ice axe for carving
a path through the cornices. When and where did equipment
and techniques begin to evolve in the present direction?

The Curve

In 1966 the American climber and equipment designer Yvon
Chouinard climber one of Europe's great ice walls, the North
Face of Les Courtes, with Layton Kor, another American. On
this climb they used front-pointing technique along with an
ice dagger and an ice axe in their hands. The security of this
sort of "clawing" was minimal, but Chouinard suggested that
in time of trouble the dagger, which should be attached by a
cord to the climber's waist, could quickly be driven in, thus
providing a makeshift belay. The future of that particular idea
was limited, but Chouinard was inspired by the climb in two

other important ways, which in retrospect *created* the future.

First, the long session of front-pointing on Les Courtes nearly destroyed Chouinard's and Kor's calf muscles. This led Chouinard to learn and adopt the French technique, which, though it is hard to master, is more relaxing on climbs that are not overly steep. More importantly, French technique forces the climber to study the ice more carefully, thus coming to know it better—the first step on the road to creative ice climbing. In the climber's mind the ice becomes a medium for expressing his art and craft rather than an enemy to be "conquered."

Secondly, Chouinard was prompted by his experience in Europe to experiment with the pick of the ice axe, allowing it to droop to make it stick better in the ice. He also added a drooped pick to his widely used "Yosemite" hammer. With one of these modified tools in each hand, normally angled ice slopes suddenly became much less difficult. And although it would be a few years before it was to happen, the way was now open for extended climbs on extremely steep and vertical ice.

In the late sixties, however, the new tools were not yet available to the public. Even so, using the old style gear, ice climbing was assuming greater and greater popularity. In Canada many excellent ice walls and glacier climbs were done, including the Northeast Face of Mount Stanley by Heins Kahl and Nick Ellena in 1966; the Delta-form Glacier by Glen Boles, Joe Farrand, Charlie Locke, and Brian Greenwood in 1968; the Northeast Face of Mount Hooker by Fred Beckey and John Rupley in 1968; the Snowbird Glacier of Mount Patterson by Ken Baker, Charlie Locke, Lloyd MacKay, Chick Scott, and Don Vockeroth; the North Face of Mount Assiniboine by Chris Jones, Chouinard, and Joe Faint in 1967; and the Northeast Face of Mount Stanley, again, but in the winter of 1969 by Urs Kallen and Eckhard Grassman. Meanwhile in America, the Black Ice Couloir was climbed several times without step-chopping; the North-side routes on Rainier began to see regular traffic; and Jim MacCarthy climbed that

Two climbers are circled on the North Face of Mount Athabasca, Canadian Rockies. This climb is typical of the sort of route that provided the challenge in the late sixties. (Photo by Jeff Lowe)

The author aid-climbing on overhanging ice on the North Face of Mount Temple, Canadian Rockies, in 1970. Today this pitch would be climbed with only the picks of two hand-tools and the front points of the crampons. (Photo by George Lowe)

old classic, Pinnacle Gully, entirely on front-points and picks, almost forty years after the first ascent.

It was from this background that ice climbing virtually exploded into the 1970s.

References

1 Blomberg, Greg. "Ice Climbing—The New Standard," *Summit*, November, 1965.
2 Chouinard, Yvon. "The North Face of Les Courtes," *American Alpine Journal*, 1967.
3 Jones, Chris. *Climbing in North America*. California: American Alpine Club, 1976.
4 MacCarthy, Jim. "Coming of Age—Ice Climbing in North America," *American Alpine Journal*, 1970.
5 Miller, Steven. Letter to the editor, *Off Belay*, August, 1972.
6 Molenaar, Dee. *The Challenge of Rainier*. Seattle: The Mountaineers, 1971.
7 Ortenberger, Leigh. *A Climber's Guide to the Teton Range*. American Alpine Club, 1965.
8 Smutek, Ray, "The Great Willis Wall Controversy," *Off Belay*.
9 Steck and Evans. "Mount Logan's Hummingbird Ridge," *American Alpine Journal*, 1966.
10 Wickwire, Jim. "Mount Rainier's Willis Wall in Winter," *American Alpine Journal*, 1971.

FROZEN WATERFALLS AND BIG EFFORTS

Scottish winter ice climbing had developed into a sport of its own as early as the 1890s, with Harold Raeburn its early inspirational figure. Since that time, winter ice climbing has been honed to a fine art in Scotland; it has a large following and much tradition. In Scotland the sport continued to grow from its inception.

Until the early 1970s in America, however, the few important climbs could be counted on the fingers of one hand: the Standard Route on Cathedral Ledge, New Hampshire, in 1956 by Stadmueller and Kendall; the Yokum Ridge on Oregon's Mount Hood in 1959 by Beckey and Schieblehener; the Northeast Face of Mount Stanley in the Canadian Rockies by Grassman and Kallen in 1969. Furthermore, we may dispense with the latter two climbs for purposes of the present discussion, as they were Alpine climbs done under winter conditions; we'll deal with them later. For now, let's trace the development in the seventies of water ice climbing on the lower crags.

Mahlen's Peak Waterfall and the Black Dike

By 1970 the new curved pick gear was available to the public. In addition, Chouinard had produced a rigid crampon without the hinge that had been a feature of the old models. Although this arrangement was not as revolutionary as the curved pick design, it did help to eliminate vibration when the front points were kicked in. It was a minor improvement on Alpine climbs but of considerable importance on water ice. With curved picks, rigid crampons, and tubular ice screws for protection, you could climb virtually any piece of ice. People were quick to try out the new gear.

In the East a few moderate new climbs were made during the winter of 1970-71, but the routes, such as Pegasus on Frankenstein Cliff by Streibert and Merrit, didn't really come close to the potential of the tools. Likewise, in Montana Pat Collis, Jim Kanzler, and others found several short and moderately steep gullies in Hyalite Canyon south of Bozeman, with the 70-degree, 200-foot Green Bully being the finest. It was on an obscure waterfall on the side of Mahlen's Peak in northern Utah that a new standard of free-climbing difficulty was established.

Earlier that winter Greg Lowe had been among the party that had made the first winter ascent of the Black Ice Couloir. He had not felt comfortable on the extremely brittle ice in the

Greg Lowe on the first pitch of Mahlen's Peak Waterfall, 1971. (Photo by Lance Wilcox)

couloir and hadn't done any leading. On his return home to Ogden, Utah, he determined to learn how to deal with even the most brittle ice.

In the foothills of the Wasatch Mountains behind his house,

he found a 350-foot-high frozen waterfall that was nearly vertical at the base and had a gently overhanging bulge about 200 feet up. Each morning during the early part of March Greg made the one-hour approach in order to climb on the base of the waterfall. He was finding the limits of his equipment and pushing his strength and technique.

By the end of the month he was ready. With Rob Brown belaying and jumaring, he made the complete ascent of the waterfall in four pitches. The first was a long pitch, averaging 80 degrees, on which he felt very confident. This was followed by a short stretch of lower angle. The third pitch was the

George Lowe during the first complete ascent of the Black Ice Couloir in 1966. (Photo by Mike Lowe)

Greg Lowe, who set a new standard of free-climbing difficulty on ice. (Photo by Jeff Lowe)

bulge he had seen from the ground. Screwing up his courage, he launched out into the unknown. Over a distance of 75 feet of vertical and overhanging ice he managed to place only a few screws for protection. The only aids he had used were the front-points of his crampons and the picks of his tools. His training had paid off; the climb was technically as hard or harder than the most difficult ice climbs in Scotland.

Later that year another bold adventure into the world of winter climbing took place. The Black Dike of Cannon Cliff in New Hampshire becomes a 600-foot ribbon of ice under winter conditions. For New England, the setting is about as Alpine and remote as you can get. The weather can be atrocious, with high winds, below-zero temperatures, and heavy snowfalls. The climb had been discussed for years, but it remained for John Bouchard to crack the aura surrounding it.

John Bouchard made a psychological breakthrough with his solo climb of the Black Dike. (Photo by John Roskelley)

Early in December, 1971, as soon as the Dike was iced sufficiently for climbing, Bouchard set out, armed with a few pitons and a rope but otherwise alone! Several hours later he arrived at the top of this cliff, which had impressed one of America's best mountaineers as "a black filthy icicle 600 feet high." Once again, as had happened 10 years before on the Willis Wall of Mount Rainier, a solitary climber succeeded on a route that had cowed the best rope teams. This time, however, the climbing community was ready to accept and learn from the progress that had been made.

The winter of 1972-73 was a time of maturing techniques and consolidating gains. Several good climbs were done in the Canadian Rockies, notably the right-hand icefall on the south side of Mount Bourgeau by Brian Greenwood, George Homer, and Rob Wood. This 1,200-foot climb required 2 days and was compared to the hardest Scottish winter routes. The climbers utilized the only available alternatives to curved ice axes and hammers: "Terrordactyls" had been imported from Scotland. Instead of being curved, the picks of the Terrors are straight but at an acute angle to the shaft. When compared with the curved tools in use, the results are similar; the method of placement is the only major difference.

Activity also increased in New England. With different partners, John Bragg made the first ascents of two of the most classic and difficult climbs. On Frankenstein Cliff he climbed the short but steep Dracula with A. J. LaFleur, and on Cathedral Ledge, with Rick Wilcox, he climbed the four-pitch Repentance. The small ranks of active ice climbers began to swell, but none of the new climbs was done in bolder style than the Black Dike nor did any require greater technical virtuosity than Mahlen's Peak Waterfall. The next two winters were to see advances in both respects.

Bridalveil Falls and the Widow's Tears

Mike Weis and I had been introduced to the possibilities of waterfall climbing by Greg Lowe in the winter of 1972. By December, 1973, we felt ready to try something really big. Bridalveil Falls, near Telluride, Colorado, is more than 400 feet high and in winter is comprised of bulge after bulge of icicle-draped blue ice. We decided it would be a suitable test, with the odds heavily weighted against success.

From previous experience with shorter but similar climbs, we knew that the brittle ice produced by weeks of sub-zero cold would not easily accept tube screws. But Greg Lowe solved this problem for us by loaning half a dozen homemade chrome-molly tubes, with tips bevelled to the inside. These

Bridalveil Falls, Telluride, Colorado. (Photo by Mike Lowe)

could be placed without completely fracturing the ice, and what's more, they could be pounded in. This latter feature is very important on long, steep leads where the length of time spent placing tools is a major component of the difficulty. The only drawback to these tubes was the need for chopping to get them out.

Mike Weis leading the crux of Bridalveil Falls on the first ascent, January 2, 1974. (Photo by Jeff Lowe)

I belayed Mike on the crux of the climb, which was a 3-foot roof of ice with giant icicles drooping from the lip. For 20 feet he climbed a slightly overhanging wall below the bulge, relying only on the picks of his tools and the front-points of his crampons for purchase. He knocked a hole in the curtain of icicles with his axe. Then he stemmed delicately against the remaining stumps on either side of the hole, swung his axe into the ice above the overhang, and muscled his way up. To this day that pitch is the hardest I have seen on any ice climb. Weis led it brilliantly.

When we arrived at the top, we were both laughing and

Mike Weis climbed Bridalveil Falls and the Grand Central Couloir. (Photo by Jeff Lowe)

The author just past the crux of Bridalveil Falls during the first climb in 1974. (Photo by Mike Weis)

amazed at our success. Where formerly we would have guessed that it was necessary to use aid stirrups attached to ice screws on a climb such as Bridalveil, we now knew that we never again would have to consider such encumbrances. But Bridalveil is a short climb, requiring ten hours on the first ascent. The next winter, high-standard free climbing was used to extend the climb to more than one day.

The Widow's Tears

By early winter 1975, Mark Chapman and Kevin Worral could each lay claim to only one or two ice climbs. But they were among the best young rock climbers in their adopted home: Yosemite Valley. They decided to gain experience at ice climbing as well, so that winter they made the first ascent of

Mark Chapman, whose ascent of the Widow's Tears with Kevin Worral in 1975 was a great adventure.

Sentinel Falls, whose 400 feet of steep water ice would have challenged the most experienced "icemen." With their short "apprenticeship" out of the way, they set their sights on a 1,000-foot runnel of ice known as the Widow's Tears.

Chapman and Worral made five attempts and returned to the valley floor each time, rebuffed by warm weather and rotten ice. On their sixth try their patience and persistence were rewarded. They found climbable conditions, but only barely. During the afternoon of the first day they had to hide under an overhang while chunks of ice went buzzing past their lair. The next day they progressed to a large ledge at the base of the final step. They shivered through another night in their meager bivouac gear.

The final day started with joy at the prospect of success by evening. Then Chapman took a 30-foot fall while leading above the ledge, and the joy turned to fear and despair. The climbers gathered their wits and courage together, however, and by evening they arrived at the top, if not in triumphant splendor, at least with satisfaction of a great adventure safely completed.

Since the climbs of Bridalveil Falls and the Widow's Tears, no new climbs have been made that require greater technical or psychological commitment. Many *comparable* climbs have been done, but it would be too cumbersome to record them all here. The coldest sport is now so popular that dozens of excellent new climbs are made each winter.*

---

*It would be irresponsible to leave this discussion without a quick survey of the best climbs made in the Canadian Rockies, for they represent the largest locale for big, winter ice climbs on the continent. In geographical order, north to south, they are:

1. The Weeping Wall: Rob Wood, George Homer, and Bugs McKeith, 1973. 600 feet at an average angle of 75 degrees. First free ascent by Dave Wright and Greg Davis, 1976.

2. Polar Circus: Adrian and Alan Burgess with Charlie Porter and Bugs McKeith, 1975. Perhaps the longest climb of its sort yet done in Canada. First free-climbed in 1978 by Jack Roberts and Dale Bard.

3. Takkakkaw Falls: Auger, McKeith, and Wood, 1974. The classic Canadian waterfall climb. First free ascent made in 1976 by Dave Wright and Duncan Ferguson.

4. Nemesis: Bugs McKeith and Dick Howe, 1974. The most technically difficult Canadian route. Has no free ascent at this writing.

5. Bourgeau Left-Hand: Tim Auger, George Homer, Rob Wmod, 1973. Another 600-foot climb, but steeper and harder than the Weeping Wall. First free ascent in 1975 by John Roskelly and partner.

So far we have spoken only of water ice; now let's take a look at the Alpine half of the game.

The North Face of Mount Fay and the Search for Difficulty

Climbers were quick to adapt to the greater possibilities offered by the new curved gear. Since old-style climbs were easier with the improved equipment, harder climbs were sought to keep the interest up. Chouinard, the main cause of all the ruckus, was himself involved in one of the first searches for technical difficulty. In 1970 Pete Carman, Dennis Eberl, and Chouinard found an ice bulge on the North Face of Mount Fay in the Canadian Rockies that offered eight pitches of much steeper climbing than that usually found on Alpine routes. Carman described the climbing:

Dave Wright's recent free ascents of the Weeping Wall, Takkakkaw Falls, and other big Canadian winter climbs have set a new trend toward a less cumbersome style of climbing. (Photo by Jeff Lowe)

"The ice changed continuously in texture, ranging from Nirvana Neve to black ice overlaid by a loosely attached layer of brittle ice, and it was consistently steep, with bulges of 70 degrees. Large bulges occupied the better part of a rope length, not the two- or three-step variety found in couloirs back East."

Another way to increase difficulty, or at least commitment, is to seek out longer routes. The same year that Mount Fay was climbed, Chris Jones and Gray Thompson succeeded on the 5,000-foot North Face of Mount Columbia. They had three days of typical Alpine ice climbing, except for one pitch in an ice-filled chimney that connects the lower icefield of the face with the upper. That pitch was more like a hard Scottish gully. Their last bivouac was in a storm, and their lightweight

Art Higbee leads the "Scottish" gully between the icefields on Mount Columbia's North Face during the third ascent. (Photo courtesy of Art Higbee)

gear did not fully insulate them from its fury. But Jones took comfort in the knowledge that "Gray's solid; we will be OK whatever we have to do; we've been through as bad before."

Columbia was the first of the really big Canadian ice faces to feel front-points and picks. Others followed in rapid

The North Face of Mount Kitchener, first climbed in 1971. (Photo by Jeff Lowe)

succession: the North Face of Mount Kitchener via the Ramp Route, a 3,500-foot climb, somewhat harder than Coluvbia, done in 1971 by Jones and Thompson accompanied by this writer; the North Face of Mount Bryce by Jim Jones and Eckhard Grassman in 1972; the Deltaform Ice Couloir, 1973,

Gray Thompson near the top of the right-hand icefield on Mount Kitchener in 1971. (Photo by Chris Jones)

by Chris Jones and George Lowe, one of the longest pure gully climbs available in the Rockies; and the Grand Central Couloir on Mount Kitchener, climbed by Mike Weis and this writer—the hardest of all the big Canadian climbs, exposed to rockfall and avalanche and requiring climbing at night to avoid the danger.

There are two other ways to increase the difficulties of an Alpine climb. One is to go in winter, when temperatures are lower and the ice is very brittle, and the other is to go alone.

The winter ascent of the Willis Wall already has been mentioned in connection with Charlie Bell's first climb of the face. But the four-day effort of Wickwire and Burtulis on the Wall should be emphasized because of the climbers' willingness to approach such a large winter problem in a lightweight Alpine style at a time when most climbers saw even easy

The Black Ice Couloir in winter, 1971. (Photo by Greg Lowe)

One way to increase the difficulty of a climb is to go alone. (Photo courtesy of Art Higbee)

winter routes as awesome. Later winter ice climbs included the Black Ice Couloir the year after the Willis Wall by four Lowes, including George, Dave, Greg and myself, and the Ramp Route on Mount Kitchener by Jim Elzinga and Eckhard Grassman in the winter of 1976. On all of these winter climbs the climbers had to deal with much harsher conditions than are found in summer. In fact, the differences are sometimes so great that the same route seems a totally new climb.

Those climbers who have become experienced in the difficulties of waterfall ice climbing have grown confident enough on normal Alpine climbs to dispense with the rope and climb solo. The summer following his ascent of Mahlen's Peak Waterfall, Greg Lowe climbed the Black Ice Couloir in less than three hours by himself. In the Canadian Rockies it became a fairly common occurrence for the milder ice faces to be soloed. The climbs around the Columbia Icefields especially saw a lot of individual activity. The North and Kain Faces of Mount Robson were both the subjects of solitary climbs, and the hardest new route in the Tetons (the Run-Don't-Walk-Couloir) fell prey to the lonely blade in July, 1976.

The hardest Teton ice route, the Run-Don't-Walk Couloir on Mount Owen. Mike Lowe soloed this route in July, 1976, ostensibly to test the new Hummingbird ice tools. (Photo by Jim Knight)

With so many climbs, so many styles, and so many climbers today, what is left for tomorrow? After all the waterfalls, Alpine faces, couloirs, iced-up rock climbs, and winter ascents what more could there be? Certain recent climbs have given us a sense of what is to come. These are: the six-day, Alpine-style climb of the South Face of Mount McKinley by Dougal Haston and Doug Scott; Charlie Porter's amazing solo of the Cassin Ridge of McKinley; Chas Macquarie and Dakers Gowan's fifteen-day, Alpine-style ascent of the North Face of Mount Deborah; and George Lowe and Mike Kennedy's fast two-day climb of the Northwest Spur of Mount Hunter.

Whatever the future holds, we should not forget our roots. Bill Summer, reflecting on several Alpine-style ice climbs he made in Alaska in 1974, perhaps has written the perfect blueprint for the future:

> The essence of Alpinism has always been a commitment to the unknown—following time's arrow along its only path. And great routes follow the mountain's natural path. And good climbs are those following these one-way paths with an irreducible minimum of equipment.

The south side of Denali (Mount McKinley) with the Cassin Ridge prominent. The British Direct route takes the sunlit slope to the right of the Cassin. (Photo by Jeff Lowe)

I would only add that, as Jonathan Swift said, "Vision is the art of seeing things invisible." The natural path is wherever you perceive it to be.

References

1 Carman, Pete. "The North Face of Mt. Fay," *American Alpine Journal*, 1971.
2 Cleare, John. *Mountains.* London: Macmillan, 1975.
3 Cole and Wilcox. "Shades of Blue," *Eastern Mountain Sports*, 1976.
4 Jones, Chris. "Mt. Columbia from the North," *American Alpine Journal*, 1971.
5 Sumner, Bill. "Ice is Nice and Will Suffice," *Ascent*, 1974.
6 Wickwire, Jim. "Mount Rainier's Willis Wall in Winter," *American Alpine Journal*, 1971.

2

The Hazards and the Gear

If anything can be said to distinguish the character of climbing in North American from climbing in Europe, it would be that Americans often are more concerned with equipment than with personal performance and that we have a more conservative attitude regarding objective dangers. These two factors have both good points and bad. The gear mania has prompted innovations that have proven their value over the years, but it also has spawned a breed of climbers whose joy in owning the latest piece of technological wizardly is greater than its love for the mountains. Similarly, the overriding concern for safety perhaps has kept the accident rate down, but at the same time it can be blamed for the stringent regulations governing climbing in our national parks.

We should learn to strike a balance. Safety is important, but freedom is valuable, too—let those who want to meet the hazards of the mountain do so on their own terms. Better equipment allows us to stretch our technical horizons. But senseless proliferation of gadgets should not continue to the point where the beauty of the hills becomes threatened by an "effluent" society.

HAZARDS OF THE COLD ROAD

Sometimes, to do an important climb one must go beyond the laws of safety and trust the percentage—in short, gamble.

—Fred Beckey
Challenge of the North Cascades

What Fred Beckey says is true, but only appropriate for climbers such as he, who have the necessary years of experience with the hazards of climbing to make an accurate assessment of the "percentage." A man such as Fred would never gamble on something he didn't *know*. Beckey would search out what has been written on the subject first, perhaps spend some time with one who knows more than he, and then very cautiously begin to see how closely this new-found theoretical information coincides with his own subsequent observations in the field. For Fred Beckey there have been no ill-considered confrontations with oblivion but rather a series of forays toward the "edge," with the security of a belay fashioned from time-tempered knowledge. His almost incident-free, 40-year career speaks eloquently of that. Such a record is worthy of emulation.

What *are* the hazards of ice climbing? How can you avoid or lessen exposure to them? The following information is only an introduction.

Avalanches

Perhaps avalanches are the most pervasive of all hazards associated with ice climbing since most ice climbs are found at the bottom of avalanche paths or are the actual paths themselves. A knowledge of the metamorphic and mechanical phenomena associated with snow and avalanches is essential, then, if you are to make the correct decision about when and where to go climbing. You'll do well to get a copy of Edward LaChappele's little booklet "The ABCs of Avalanche Safety," and study it thoroughly. It contains the very minimum of information with which an ice climber should be familiar. A few of the factors that go into determining avalanche hazard are:

1) The steepness and configuration of the slope. Convex slopes, which are under tension, are more likely to slide than concave slopes, which gravity tends to compact. Slopes with inclines greater than 30 degrees are always suspect, though twice in Canada I have seen an entire winter's snow-pack suddenly let loose on angles no greater than 10 degrees. This shows that not only the angle is important but the nature of the underlying surface as well. The slides in Canada both occurred in early summer on bare rock slabs that were well-lubricated by running water.

2) The composition of the snow pack, old and new. Each successive snowfall will bond to some degree with the surface of the old snow underneath. If the underlying surface is ice, the bond will, of course, be insubstantial but not necessarily untrustworthy. If the new snow is deposited at near-freezing temperatures, it will have a chance to freeze onto the ice. If the temperature drops substantially after this initial bond has been made, it's a good sign, as the bond will be further set. The opposite will be true, however, when a storm starts out cold and gets warmer. Beware of this development.

The speed at which snow falls is a factor in predicting the probability of avalanches also. Whenever there is a deposition rate of a couple of inches or more per hour, you can bet on at least some snow sluffing. Many small sluffs, however, without triggering a large slide, are an indication that the slope is stabilizing itself.

If winds greater than a few knots per hour are present during a storm, wind slabs will form, and these are very unstable. In fact, any time the wind moves snow around, slabs

A new snow sluff avalanche down the line of an ice-filled chimney in Colorado. (Photo by Jeff Lowe)

will develop on lee slopes and in shallow depressions, gullies, etc. In the Rocky Mountains in winter, slabs often are triggered by the collapse of a weak layer somewhere in the snowpack. This weakness is formed during long spells of clear, cold weather. At such times there is a great difference in the temperature of the snow at the surface compared to subsequent layers, and moisture is leached from a strata of the snow-pack. This creates long, cylindrical crystals that do not intermesh well. This temperature gradiant (TG) snow commonly is known as "depth hoar," and it can be spotted easily if you dig a pit through the winter's snow-pack and look for a layer of sugar-like granules that crumble at a touch. In springtime (all summer in some ranges) you can expect wet snow avalanches. These usually can be avoided by climbing at night or early morning. This assumes, of course, that the temperature drops low enough to firm up the snow.

By now it should be obvious that so many variables govern avalanche prediction that caution always should be the order of the day. Whenever there is any question, stay out of gullies or couloirs and stick to ridges or ribs on a face.

Cornices

On ridges you'll face another problem in the form of wind-formed lips of snow, which can give way spontaneously or under the weight of a climber. Stay on the windward side of these cornices, below the potential fracture line, which often is lower than you might first guess. Once you are actually on a cornice, it's hard to estimate the area of probably collapse, so look ahead, and plan your route well in advance.

Crevasses

If, during the course of your climbing career, you travel extensively on glaciers, the odds are overwhelmingly good that at one time or another (probably *several* times) you will find yourself plummeting into the jaws of a crevasse. Proper management of the rope will hold the fall to a minimum

*Crevasses and an icefall
on a glacier in Alaska.
(Photo by Jeff Lowe)*

distance, and prior practice of rescue techniques (self-rescue and rescue by others of an injured climber) will reduce the length of time spent in the icy bowels of the mountain. *Mountaineering: The Freedom of the Hills* is one of the best sources of information on these topics. As a rule, traveling against the general crevasse pattern is safer than parallel to it because there is less chance of more than one climber falling in at the same time.

Weather

"The wonder of a single snowflake outweighs the wisdom of a million meteorologists," said Francis Bacon. Where there's ice, there's inclement weather—it's as simple as that. A true ice climber appreciates that fact and learns to live with it, making the decision to retreat or go on in the face of an oncoming storm with no regrets or self-chastisement even when the

Climbing in a snowstorm. (Photo by Mike Kennedy)

clouds suddenly clear just as the last man is off the last rappel or when, as the storm increases in ferocity after the route has been pushed beyond retreat, he must endure a frigid bivouac. In the high mountains of North America, major storms normally are preceded by streaks of high, "serious" (cirrus) clouds that give a six- to 24-hour warning.

"Winter is not a season, it is an occupation," according to Sinclair Lewis.

Falling Ice and Rock

The leader often breaks off chunks of ice while he is climbing, much to the dismay of those below him. For that reason, always attempt to make diagonal leads so that anything

Ice climbers learn to accept storms as part of the ice experience. (Photo by George Lowe)

knocked down will not threaten the belayer. Warm weather or sunshine (or both) can weaken the ice, causing large icicles to fall or the entire structure on which one is climbing to collapse. The quality of the ice-to-rock bond is a function of temperature and type of rock. On a mild day ice might stick solidly to porous limestone but fall off of glacier-polished granite. Loose rocks that are held in place only by the ice around them also might fall. A helmet is no protection against anything very big.

These two views of Bridalveil Falls, photographed during different seasons, illustrate the changing nature of ice climbs. Note the increased amount of ice in the second photo. (First photo by Greg Lowe; second, by Jeff Lowe)

Falling Climber

Though protection techniques are now quite advanced and generally reliable, the sharp tools that adorn the ice climber are likely to do considerable damage even in a short fall. There is an old adage that many of today's rock climbers scoff at but which the budding ice climber would do well to revere: "The leader must not fall."

Low Temperatures

Frostbite and hypothermia are real possibilities, even with the best clothes, as the ice climber is by definition out in the coldest weather, and positions that hamper circulation sometimes must be maintained for long periods of time. Always carry more clothes than you'll need to wear while you're active and some high calorie foods such as maragine and Logan Bread.

THE SOFT SIDE OF ICE

Doug Robinson, the "Gnome of California" (High Sierra) ice climbing, on everything-the-well-dressed-and-equipped-ice-climber-needs: "The ice climber, once he is done up from head to ankles in wool, need only add a pair of high quality mountaineering boots, rigid front-point crampons, ice axe, Alpine hammer, and a flask of straight malt Scotch."[1] What's this? Tom Patey reincarnated as a five-foot-four Hermit of the Sierras[2] No, just an example of the way spirits tend to rise when you're having fun with ice. And a good description of the well-equipped ice-person. But if that is not enough, then some specifics will follow.

---

1. "Ascent," *Sierra Club Mountaineering Journal*, 1971, p.37.
2. Tom Patey was one of Scotland's most influential ice climbers. He once said: "Ice is for pouring whiskey on."

To avoid sounding like a lecture from your mother when you were ten years old, this discussion is limited to apparel that has a specific use regarding ice climbing and to the special problems that confront the climber who ventures out in the harsh environment.

Basic Clothing

Wool, with its property of remaining warm even when damp, is an excellent natural material for socks, pants, underwear, hats, mittens, gloves, sweaters, etc. However, experience has shown certain synthetic materials to be more effective than wool when used in the same garments. Many expeditions, beginning with the 1969 British expedition to the South Face of Annappurna, have used synthetic-pile clothing. The climbers involved have reported that this works well under adverse conditions. The choice between wool and synthetics, then, is one of aesthetics more than of function.

Until recently, the ice climber has had to face the paradoxical question: is it good to leave your wool clothing uncovered to allow body moisture to pass out through the pores of the cloth even though you will get soaked when you're forced to come into intimate contact with the snow? Or is it better to put on coated nylon over-clothes, thus keeping the snow out but, unfortunately, trapping body moisture within? This dilemma now has been solved with the introduction of a new treatment for nylon fabric called Gore-Tex®. This Teflon-type coating has millions of tiny pores that allow moisture to pass through from the warmer side (next to your body) to the colder side (the outside air) while effectively stopping the passage of moisture in the opposite direction. It's a welcome, if expensive, boon to all outdoors people. Not the least to benefit is the ice climber.

If Gore-Tex® is too expensive, wind pants and parkas of uncoated nylon shed snow well and preserve body heat in dry and/or windy conditions; the porosity of uncoated material lets moisture escape. But the wet winters of the Pacific Northwest and California might require coated outer clothing.

Parkas and Sleeping Bags

Down, down. Always goose down for duvets and bags. In our minds it has been ingrained that down is the warmest per weight of any available insulating material. But down is notoriously bad in damp conditions.

Years ago we snickered and called Petzoldt eccentric, maybe even senile for outfitting his winter expeditions to the Tetons with Dacron-filled sleeping bags. Then we went there ourselves and lived in tiny snow caves in the Black Ice Couloir. Our breath, body heat, and stoves melted the sides of the caves, and it was impossible to keep our down bags from touching them. After a couple of nights we were soaked; one of us was weak from lack of sleep; our bags were reduced to frozen clumps of down between nylon sheets. The storm raged heavy. We forgot the summit and made a descent in darkness from the Upper Saddle. We finally reached the guide's hut on the Lower Saddle. Another night in snow caves would have been unpleasant at best. The door of the hut was ajar and snow had blown in, covering the floor. In one corner were several Dacron-filled sleeping bags, frozen solid and stuck together like a catch of trout in the freezer. Skeptically, we pried them apart and crawled in. In half an hour the bags were dry next to our bodies, and we slept warm.

That was several years ago. Synthetic fillings have been improved since then. Products such as Dupont's Fiberfill II® and Fortrel's Polarguard® are only about 25 percent heavier and bulkier than down when compressed. Sleeping bags and parkas filled with this kind of insulation lose very little loft when wet, and they dry quickly. If you think you might encounter worse than ideal conditions, synthetic fillings deserve your consideration.

Gore-Tex®-covered down gear is an alternative to synthetic-filled clothing. This type of garment works well in all but the wettest conditions. There are times when even small savings of weight and space can be crucial, justifying the high price.

Footwear

The easiest way to get cold feet is to wear tight boots or too many socks in boots that otherwise would fit well. Even double boots won't keep your feet warm if circulation is impaired. Soft boots that crush under crampon straps will cause cold feet in the same way. A hard, round toe (German style), whether your boots are double or single, is much warmer than a narrow (French style) toe. For good crampon control, it is only necessary for boots to fit snugly around the ankle, heel, and instep. Stiff soles help relieve fatigue in the calf muscles when front-pointing on steep ice. Rigid frame crampons *require* stiff-soled boots to avoid overstressing the steel. Make certain the boots you buy are made specifically for *heavy-duty climbing*—don't settle for a pair of hunting paks suggested by a pushy salesman! Gaiters are needed to keep snow out of the boots.

There are several kinds of sole-less, insulated overboots commercially available in North America. These attach to the welt of the boot by different methods. With the sole exposed, there is no need for removal if rock is encountered, as is the case with full overboots. A single boot with the addition of a "supergaiter" often has greater insulation thickness than a double mountaineering boot and will, therefore, keep your feet warmer.

Helmets, Face Masks, Goggles, and Dark Glasses

Wearing a helmet while climbing steep, brittle, winter ice is as important as wearing a helmet while climbing on steep, rotten rock. In his attempts to plant his tools in the ice, the leader often knocks off chunks of ice large enough to crack the belayer's skull, no matter how thick that might be. You must balance your feeling for freedom with your instinct for survival, and decide for yourself whether or not to wear a helmet.

In the mountains of North America winter winds are often extreme, whipping snowflakes along at blinding speeds and searing exposed parts of the face. Without goggles in such a storm, the climber can see no better than a rhinoceros in a sandstorm. And without a windproof face mask, frostbite can be expected because of the already low temperature coupled with the wind-chill. If you plan an extended climb in the winter mountains, it is advisable to carry these two items. Dark glasses should always be carried—the darker the better since snow reflects sunlight like a mirror. The glasses should be "polarized" and have shields on the temples to reduce glare from the sides.

In order to avoid rockfalls or avalanches that occur later in the day, it is sometimes necessary to start a climb in the dark so that you are above the danger zone before the sun hits the top of the climb. If you make an ascent in the dark, you'll need a headlamp. Mountain Safety Research sells the best one. The lithium batteries seem overly expensive at first, but the savings in weight and longevity more than make up for the added cost. As an example, regular alkaline batteries will have to be changed at least once during the course of a 12-hour night while the same headlamp powered by lithium batteries will last at least three or four nights.

Bivouac Considerations

Bivouacs on snow and ice are not much different from bivouacs on rock—just a little colder. The most important item of gear for such a bivouac is a good closed-cell foam pad of one-half inch or greater thickness to eliminate the heat loss caused by close contact with snow or ice. For bivouac sacks and tents, Gore-Tex® is once again an almost revolutionary answer to the age-old problem of "coated or uncoated." The

A winter bivouac in the Black Ice Couloir. (Photo by Greg Lowe)

same principles that apply to outer clothing apply here. Just remember to seal the seams of any Gore-Tex® article with special Gore-Tex® seam sealer (called Seam Stuff); ordinary seam sealant does not stick well to the coating. It's amazing how wet you can get through untreated seams alone.

NECESSITIES AND TRINKETS

There is such a large variety of ice climbing gear available these days that it would be too cumbersome to list every brand, model, and style. But a discussion of desirable characteristics, materials, and designs for each item is appropriate to help you make decisions when you set out to acquire your kit. One or two examples of acceptable brands will be given for each item. This does not mean, however, that a brand not mentioned is inferior.

Crampons

There are crampons available that do not have two points protruding out from the toe of the boot, but we are concerned only with those that do—the "twelve-point" sort. Many of the techniques described later would be impossible without them.

The main body, or frame, of the crampon either can be hinged at a point under the arch of the foot, or it can be rigid from toe to heel. Hinged crampons—Salewa makes them—can be used successfully on ice of any angle but require greater ankle and calf strength when used for front-pointing on steep ice. On the other hand, rigid crampons, such as Chouinard or SMC, allow you to keep your heels low in relation to your toes, transferring the strain from the muscles of the calf to the tendons of the ankle and heel; these tendons are well suited to holding a static load, such as that applied when a climber is "resting" between moves on steep ice. Another advantage of a rigid frame is that it vibrates less when the front-points are kicked into the ice. That is particularly important on the brittle water ice that is commonly the medium for climbing in

North American winters—vibration can shatter the ice around the front-points, making their purchase shaky.

It makes little sense to own more than a single pair of crampons. One pair of the adjustable kind will fit summer or winter boots and work as well for glacier walking as for climbing vertical, frozen waterfalls. The days of heating and bending crampon frames to each new pair of boots have given way to simple adjustments made with a screwdriver or wrench. For maximum control, crampons should be adjusted so that they will stay on the boot without straps when lifted up.

Front-points should extend about three-fourths to one inch in front of the boot. Generally speaking, the harder the ice, the less the front-points should protrude. An exception should be made on steep waterfalls with surfaces consisting of icicles and air—keep your points long in this instance if you wish to avoid the feeling that you are climbing with roller skates. The front-points should be adjusted short for iced-up rock. The other ten points should follow with some accuracy the outline of your boot sole. Fit your crampons to your boots as carefully as you would fit ski boots to bindings, for the nuances of control are similar.

Front-points on crampons come in two configurations: they might be curved in a downward arc, as are SMC and Chouinard, or they might be set at an angle of about 45 degrees (Salewa hinged). The points may be in either a horizontal or vertical plane. Both curved points and those that are bent at an angle allow one to relax the legs by dropping the heels; the points will still bite. Front-points whose wide dimension is in a vertical plane are bad because they might shear through soft ice or hard snow.

A secure arrangement for strapping crampon to boot is of primary importance. That might sound like advice for an idiot, but many experienced climbers have lost a crampon in the middle of a climb. Somehow it "just fell off." There are several things you can do to lessen the chances of finding yourself in this precarious and embarrasing situation: 1) Use straps with positive buckles, i.e., buckles with pins that go through a hole in the strap, making it virtually impossible for the strap to slip. 2) If your boots have a very low ankle, don't wrap the rear strap around the ankle of the boot—it might slip above the boot, causing excess slack; instead, go directly over the instep with the strap and straight to the buckle. 3) After crossing the toe of the boot diagonally with the front strap, come *up* through the front-strap ring of the crampon, then pass the end of the strap *behind* the diagonal part of the strap before threading it through the opposite strap ring. This will keep the strap from sliding off the front of the boot toe. The best straps are made of neoprene-coated nylon—they don't get wet and freeze, which makes removing the crampons a chore. Beck is one of the best brands.

Several different bindings have been developed for crampons. They attach to the welt of the boot, often in a manner similar to ski bindings. Tpeir use is not yet widespread though there are obvious advantages: ease in getting the crampons on and off and no pressure over the toe and instep to collapse the boot and restrict circulation. Bindings currently available require boots with a pronounced welt.

Ice Axe

The ice axe is the climber's primary hand tool. In Kubrick's movie *2001: A Space Odyssey* a pre-man used a thigh bone as a club, and with this crude weapon he dominated his fellow apes. A simple discovery, yet it revolutionized his world. The traditional straight-pick ice axe is not far different from a bone used as a tool. Smashing away at the ice—chopping steps in the face of the enemy-mountain—seems outdated and is.

A simple curve is all that is needed. Nothing fancy, just a pick curved to match the arc of the swing. All the force is concentrated at the point of the pick; there's a sound "thunk," and the pick penetrates solidly. The axe locks when you pull out on the handle, and it hooks when you pull down. The

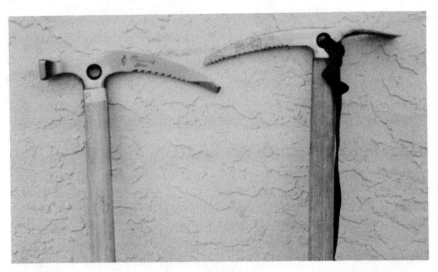

*If the pick of your ice axe is shaped like the one at left, it will tend to
skate on the surface of thin ice or during self-arrest on very hard snow.
It should be filed to the shape of the pick at right to give it bite under
those conditions. (Photo by Jeff Lowe)*

curved-pick ice axe has revolutionized ice climbing. When we
talk about ice axes in this book, we are referring only to those
with usable curves, such as the Chouinard "pidet," or drooped
blades, as on the MacInnes-Peck (the pick is straight but set at
an acute angle to the shaft, forming a hook that performs
similarly to the curved pick except for the locking action). An
ice axe has a curved or drooped pick, an adze for cutting, a
shaft of wood or metal, and a spike at the end of the shaft.

The adze of an ice axe may be flat or cupped; a flat adze
with sharp corners seems to work best for cutting. An adze
angled down toward the shaft of the axe makes cutting
difficult as the force of the blow from such an axe hits the ice
at an angle. Therefore, it's best to choose an axe with an adze
that protrudes nearly straight out from the shaft. A wavy edge
on the adze offers no discernable advantage, and it makes
sharpening unnecessarily difficult.

Should the shaft be hickory or metal tubing? Should it be
fiberglass-wrapped or laminated bamboo? All of these mate-

rials for ice-axe shafts have their advocates. Straight-grained hickory is nice to feel and look at and strong enough for ice axe use if one carries a deadman for belays on snow. Metal is strong enough for snow belays, but ice-axe belays are untrustworthy anyway. (It's better to use a deadman.) Fiberglass is also strong, but it adds weight to the shaft, affecting the balance of the axe. Laminated bamboo is consistently as strong as the best hickory, yet it is lighter and the grain raises with wear to improve the grip. Make your own choice of shaft material, but learn the strengths and weaknesses of the material you choose, and don't ask it to perform beyond those boundaries.

The cross-section shape of all good ice-axe shafts is roughly oval. This helps the climber orient the pick or adze during the swing. The spike at the end of the shaft should be firmly anchored to the shaft, for it often is relied upon in French technique.

On steep ice a sling of half-inch webbing can take much of the strain off the arms. If the head of your axe has a carabiner hole, anchor the sling there and make a loop in the other end that reaches just above the spike. Make certain the loop is large enough to allow your mittened hand to slip in and out easily. If your axe lacks a carabiner hole, you'll have to devise another means of securing the sling to the head, near the shaft. (Wrist loops will be discussed in greater depth in the next chapter.)

Extra teeth behind the normal ones on the pick of the axe will make climbing more secure on steep ice or thin ice with a hollow behind it. Such thin ice often is found on frozen waterfalls and is made of clumps of icicles that gradually have formed into a solid-looking but air-pocketed mass. The extra teeth can be shallower than the normal ones. If you make them too large, the pick will be hard to wrench from the ice. They should be put in with a bastard file to avoid ruining the temper of the steel. Certain axes come smiling from the factory with all the teeth already in their heads. The end of the pick should be shaped as in the illustration to avoid an "ice skate" effect during self-arrest and on very thin ice.

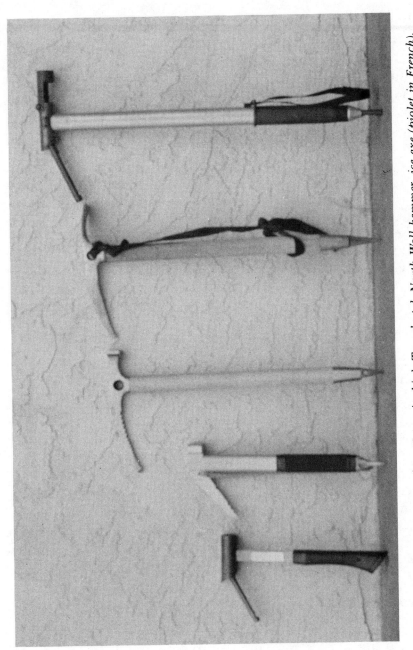

Types of hand-tools. From left: Hummingbird, Terrodactyl, North Wall hammer, ice axe (piolet in French), Big Bird (prototype ice tool from Lowe Alpine Systems). (Photo by Jeff Lowe)

Alpine Hammer; North Wall Hammer; The Hummingbird

For placing ice pitons and as a companion tool to the ice axe on extreme ice, you'll need one of these tools. An Alpine hammer has a shorter pick than an ice axe (with a curve or droop), a hammer head, and no spike at the end of a short handle. A North Wall hammer (also called a "Zero" and "Terrordactyl" in the illustration) is best pictured as a short axe with a hammer head in place of the adze. Again, shaft material and length are matters of individual preference. As with ice axes, extra teeth in the pick are needed. A sling for a North Wall hammer can be made and attached as for an ice axe.

Lowe Alpine Systems recently has introduced an Alpine hammer, called the "Hummingbird," with a tubular pick. This greatly reduces chances of fracturing brittle ice because all of the force of the blow is directed *in* toward the center of the tube rather than *out* and into the ice. The company also is experimenting with the same concept applied to ice axes and North Wall hammers ("Big Bird" in illustration).

Sharpening Hand- and Foot-Tools

Always keep the points of your tools sharp. Then, rather than bludgeoning the ice, they will penetrate easily, adding greatly to your security. Use a hand file to protect the temper of the steel. File the front-points of crampons down (in the direction of the curve or angle) on the top side; that limits conflicting forces when kicking them in. In general, let the shape of all points as they came from the factory be your guide when resharpening. On long climbs where considerable rock might be encountered it's a good idea to carry a small file for touch-ups on the go.

General Care of Gear

Keep the shafts of all wood axes sealed against water absorbtion, using a 50-50 mixture of turpentine and linseed oil; or use pine tar and apply with heat from a hand torch as you would treat the bottoms of cross-country skis. Cross-country waxes can be used on shafts to increase grip. A thin coating of oil on the metal parts of axes and crampons, applied before storage, will keep rust to a minimum. Before each climb, check all crampons and straps, wrist loops, hammers, and axes for hairline fractures and fatigue cracks; also check Allen screws for tightness.

THE SCREW'S TURN

The advent of the tubular ice screw has raised ice protection considerably. The old adage that a poor rock piton is better than a good ice piton is no longer true. A well-placed tubular screw in good Alpine ice will hold more than 2,000 pounds of sheer force and offers considerable resistance to an outward pull. In solid water ice, tests show that tube screws will offer 4,500 pounds or more of resistance consistently!

Tube Screws

The problem with tube screws is that ice in the center of old-style screws freezes solidly to the metal. This ice must be removed before they can be redriven. It is a more difficult task than might at first be imagined. Salewa has attempted to ease this problem by cutting a slit in the shaft of their screws to relieve the pressure. But that does not alleviate freeze-up. Stubai has come out with a tube that is cut in half along its length, except near the very tip. That stops icing, but the screw is hard to place securely as it tends to widen its hole as it is being inserted.

The Great Pacific Iron Works has a tube screw very similar to the Salewa, and they have almost eliminated icing by use of a smaller inside diameter at the tip of the tube than at the end. Thus ice is forced through the small opening and can fall out the back. Mountain Safety Research has a screw with a smaller diameter and more threads per inch than either the Chouinard or Salewa tubes. This screw also has a smaller inside tip diameter, but it tends to ice up more than the

Chouinard. Extended threads on ice screws, all the way from the tip to the eye, are a good idea. They help if the hole becomes enlarged due to melt; the threads act like the teeth on the pick of an ice axe and grip just inside the entrance to the hole.

Pound-ins

There are several designs of ice screws and pitons (drivable forms of ice protection) that have a solid cross-section, unlike the tubular form. All of these designs tend to fracture the ice more than tubular screws and are therefore second best. The Salewa spiral piton (better known as a "warthog" because of its knobby appearance) is designed to be driven in with a hammer. This is a great convenience on a hard lead but is somewhat countered by the need for chopping them most of the way out before they can be unscrewed the remaining distance. Again, the Great Pacific Iron Works (Chouinard) has marketed a similar piton made of superior metal. The Nester "super piton" is a drivable solid piton designed to be screwed out. Unfortunately, it tends to fracture brittle ice even more than other solid pitons, and the smaller thread displacement causes it to be insecure if the hole enlarges through melt.

Lowe Alpine Systems has developed a tube with small threads that can be driven into ice and screwed out. It fractures the ice less than other screws, and a clearing slot allows it to be cleaned easily.

Screw-Placing Tool

A ratchet for placing screws makes the chore easier, if you want to get mechanical. One can be made by cutting a slot out of a three-fourths-inch socket and welding the socket to the face of a ratchet wrench. The slot slips over the eye of the screw. Since most ratchet wrenches work only in one direction, a second socket must be welded to the opposite side of the wrench if the tool is to be used for removing screws as well. A ratchet wrench is preferred to a reversible ratchet handle because of the hole in the wrench's head, which allows the core of ice extruded from the rear of the tube as the screw is being placed to slide out unobstructed.

Deadmen

Belays on snow are best made with "deadmen" or, on harder snow, smaller versions of the same design called "dead boys." Desirable features include a roof-bend, a cable fixed at an angle, and a reinforced pounding surface. The roof-bend causes the deadman always to present the greatest surface area to the direction of pull. The cable fixed at an angle keeps the deadman "fluking" deeper into the snow when force is applied at the cable. A reinforced pounding surface adds longevity to the life of an expensive piece of gear. Mountain Safety Research makes the best deadman.

Pickets

The relatively soft snow often found in the walls of crevasses, seracs, bergschrunds, etc., sometimes requires the use of long "snow pickets." These are aluminum stakes of various lengths with tubular, T-shaped, or V-shaped cross-sections. Normally, they are at least two feet long. SMC sells a good picket.

Snow Shovel

A shovel is used for making tent platforms, digging snow caves, and climbing on corniced ridges. Most of the commercially available snow shovels for mountaineering are too flimsy. They virtually wilt at the sight of hard snow. The only good commercial shovel is an all aluminum model by Sherpa-Tubbs. Unfortunately, only a few stores carry these, and they are expensive. A very good shovel can be made, however, from an aluminum grain scoop. Cut the blade down about three inches and shorten the handle to about two feet, but leave the D-grip in place as it will make shoveling easier. File the edge of the shovel to a sharp bevel.

3

Regimen for Snow Sloggers and Ice Dancers

A general knowledge of the hills is more important than technical proficiency with axe and crampons. Before venturing into a gully in Huntington Ravine or attempting the ascent of an ice face in the Canadian Rockies, the climber must be fully capable of recognizing avalanche potential. You must have a knowledgeable. Books are tools, as are the ice axe and cram- should know how to bivouac in a snow cave and navigate through a white-out with a compass; you'll need to know how to ski or snowshoe to reach many climbs; and you must be capable (physically and emotionally) of retreat if conditions require such a move. But how do you learn to be "at home" in the mountains—especially the cold and windy winter mountains?

You can read books. Books such as this one for specific climbing skills and books such as *Mountaineering: The Freedom of the Hills* for general mountaineering techniques (orienteering, first aid, camp craft, etc.). But reading books can

The best way to learn to ice climb is by doing it. (Photo by Mike Lowe)

only give the climber ideas. You must learn by doing. Only through a patient accumulation of experience do you become knowledgeable. Books are tools, as is the ice axe and crampons. As tools, the techniques described are meant for use in the mountains and on the ice, not in the living room by the warmth of a fire. The only warmth in the snowy mountains comes from the fire that burns within. Fuel that fire with paper and it will burn out fast, but logs of experience burn with a steady, long-lasting heat. Go slow, be cautious, and build your experience gradually.

THERE'S SNOW TECHNIQUE WORTH LEARNING

The average athlete, especially if he has scrambled amongst rocks and cliffs even on the lowest hills, requires a hundredfold less education to become safe or even expert on rocks than on snow and ice.

—James Outram
In the Heart of the Canadian Rockies

Snow climbing is the old maid sister of glamorous ascents on ice. Slogging up a low-angle snow slope, though it does require endurance and patience and is necessary on many Alpine and winter climbs, is about as enjoyable as running uphill in the sand with a pack on your back. But such efforts are a necessary evil and part of the snow art of uphill clambering.

When snow is compacted by wind, time, pressure, or any combination of a nearly infinite number of influences, it becomes a lovely and enjoyable medium of ascent. Snow climbing is a subtle art that can be as difficult (and more demanding psychologically) as pure ice climbing. For instance, when climbing a cornice of soft snow, rather than simply bashing your way up a steep slope of ice on picks and front-points, you must learn to distribute your weight among all your holds. Leigh Ortenburger said snow that "just barely sustains one's weight does not yield to French phraseology."[1]

---

1. *American Alpine Journal*, 1972, p. 37.

Opposite page: Go slow, be cautious, and build your experience gradually. (Photo by Greg Lowe)

The techniques described in this book are meant for use in the mountains and on the ice, not in the living room by the warmth of the fire. (Photo by Mike Lowe)

Self-Arrest

The self-arrest is perhaps the single most important skill in the mountaineer's repertory of ice-axe related techniques. You should not realistically consider yourself a competent snow and ice climber until you are absolutely familiar with this skill and literally can perform a self-arrest from an upside-down-and-backwards position while carrying a heavy pack. Self-arrest should be practiced on a slope with a safe run-out until it is second nature to apply it instantly should a slip occur unexpectedly. Travel on steep snow slopes in the mountains should not be undertaken until this skill is mastered.

Several of the books on the reading list at the end of Chapter 2 provide in-depth coverage of self-arrest technique and should be studied in addition to reading what follows here.

The theory of self-arrest is simple: when a slip occurs, you just drag the pick of your ice axe in the snow until you eventually come to a stop. In practice, however, there are some

Carry the axe like this to avoid injuring someone in front of or behind you when walking in a group. (Photo by John Ruger)

difficulties. The hardest but most important thing to do is to avoid losing your axe. Three things will help here:

1) Hold the axe correctly. The self-arrest position of the hands on the axe consists of one hand curled over the pick, thumb behind the shaft, in front of the adze. The other hand holds the shaft low, down near the spike. The shaft is thus held diagonally across the body, and good control can be maintained.

2) If a slip has left you on your back, grab the axe in the manner just described and *roll toward the pick*, which should be held above the shoulder on the same side of your head as the hand that is grasping it. Thus, if your right hand is on the head of the axe and your left hand is on the shaft, you should roll to the right. The reason for this is that if you roll toward the hand that holds the shaft, there is a strong likelihood that the spike will dig into the snow, and the axe will be wrenched from your grasp.

3) If a great deal of momentum has developed before you have gotten yourself into position to initiate the arrest, the pick should be inserted somewhat gradually in order to prevent the axe from being torn out of your hands. This assumes, of course, that there is time enough for this tactic since it will do you no good to apply the arrest *gradually* once you have slid over a cliff at the end of a slope.

Find a slope of hard snow with a gentle run-out to practice on. It must have a configuration such that even if you made no attempt to stop yourself, you eventually would slide to a halt on the flat, uninjured. Get rid of any wrist loops you might have on your axe. There's no need for them since the slope is safe anyway. If you lose control of the axe and it is attached to you, there is a possibility of injury. A slope with a bad run-out can be used if you belay. Don't wear your crampons during arrest practice as there is a real danger of snagging them and breaking an ankle.

Your first attempt at self-arrest should be made from a feet-first position, on your back, head uphill. Holding the axe in the arrest position, let yourself slide a bit, gaining some momentum, then *roll toward the head of the axe* and apply pressure to the pick, causing it to bite into the snow. If you spread your feet wide, you'll gain an extra measure of control. During successive practices, allow more and more momentum to develop. In very soft snow try using the adze for arrest if the pick is not stopping your slide quickly enough.

The most difficult position from which to effect an arrest is head downhill and on your back. With the axe held in arrest position, you must insert the pick alongside your body; that should slow your upper body and allow your legs to swing down the slope away from the axe. Then you are in the self-arrest position.

Route Finding on Snow

Two sets of observations are required to find the best path through snow-covered mountains. The first set is made from a distance and includes an evaluation of the obvious hazards. Is there danger from avalanche, icefall or rockfall? Are there partially hidden crevasses on a glacier? Are cornices visible from a distance that you won't be able to see once you're climbing over them? From these long-range data, you will form a general plan of attack, sometimes making the decision to climb a more difficult buttress or ridge rather than an adjacent easy gully in the interest of lessening exposure to avalanches, which you have seen periodically sweep the couloir bottom.

The second set of mental notes is made on the spot and should be taken with an eye for ease of ascent. If the slope is composed of soft snow, you can save yourself some effort by seeking out areas that appear slightly wind-blown or opaque, a little grayer than the rest; the snow in such places is often more consolidated. Though your path might wander, it's always better to take the easy way, where a steady pace can be maintained. Try to flow through the hills on a stream of intelligent decisions; the mind should work more than the body—it's stronger.

Step Kicking

Step kicking is the basic snow-climbing technique. It requires stiff boots for best results. Developing a rhythm is important, as rhythm conserves energy.

As the snow gets harder and the slope steeper, you'll find yourself leaning in and trying to get a better bite with the edge of your boot by edging harder and harder. These tendencies are wrong and ultimately will lead you to grief. The harder the snow and the steeper the slope, the more important it is to stand straight up, directly over your feet, and to keep the soles of your boots in a horizontal plane.

Often when the snow is soft an attack straight up the fall line is best while on harder snow it is easier to kick steps as you zig-zag up the hill. Always carry the axe in your uphill hand when ascending a snow slope diagonally; when you change directions, change hands. The spike of the shaft should be shoved into the snow with each step, as added security against a slip.

Kicking steps up low-angle snow. (Photo by John Ruger)

The Plunge Step

A certain amount of aggressive confidence is required to descend a moderate snow slope efficiently. If the snow is at least soft enough to form a platform for about half the sole of your boot as you step down hard, the best method of descent is known as the plunge step. The action follows the name quite closely: simply walk down the slope, facing the valley, confidently plunging the entire weight of your body onto the heel of your boot with each step. Knees must be nearly straight in order to transfer the force of the plunge directly to the snow. You must also avoid leaning back as this tends to cause the platform you have formed with your plunge to fail. Properly done, with weight directly over the feet (axe held in self-arrest position if there is any possibility of a bad fall if you slip), the plunge step has a certain stern elegance.

Glissading

The art of sliding down a snow slope in control is one of the most exhilarating of all mountaineering techniques. It is also a very hazardous activity if performed on the wrong side or under the wrong conditions. It requires experience to judge conditions correctly, but anyone can learn to spot a slope that has a safe configuration, that is, one with a good run-out and no rocks or cliffs in the way.

On low to moderately angled slopes with good snow conditions, i.e., slightly mushy corn snow, it is possible to stand with bent knees and "ski" down the slope on your boots. Control is managed by edging the boots into the snow. If you are a good skier, this type of glissade is pure fun. Linked turns can be executed and jumps can be made. Hold the ice axe in the self-arrest position, ready to stop a fall and also to control the axe so you don't accidentally stab yourself.

A glissade also can be performed in a sitting posture, controlling your speed by dragging the spike of your axe in the snow alongside your body. Once again, the hands should hold the axe in self-arrest position.

An even more undignified (but very controlled) descent can be managed on quite steep slopes by lying face down on the slope, feet downhill, and controlling your speed with the pick of your axe in the snow. You simply assume the self-arrest position from the beginning.

Experienced climbers sometimes will belay each other in leapfrog fashion down a slope with a bad run-out. But wait until ymu have had lots of experience with glissading and belaying on snow before you attempt to do this.

To descend hard slopes of steep snow, it is better to face the mountain and climb down backward. Holding the axe by the top of its head, shove the shaft into the snow as low down as you comfortably can reach (use the pick if the snow is very hard) with each step or set of steps. Kick the toes of your boots in solidly, and don't hug the slope.

Cutting Steps in Snow

Most step cutting might better be considered part of ice climbing. But there is a borderline condition when the snow is just a little too hard for good step kicking, but with one blow from the adze, a good step can be formed. This requires a technique different from most other step-cutting methods and is applicable only to snow climbing. Using the adze of the axe to cut the step, try flicking your wrist at the moment the adze enters the snow. With practice, you'll be able to form a usable step with a single blow.

Extremely Steep Slopes

On very steep slopes it is best to use a tool in each hand that has a spike at the end of a reasonably long shaft. For instance, the leader can take the second's axe as well as his own to tackle the summit cornice at the top of an Alpine ice climb. The second is then left to fend for himself or the axe is lowered on the rope if that is possible. With an axe in each hand, walls of vertical snow can be climbed. The technique is simple: alternately shove one shaft and then the other into the snow as deeply as possible, angling them down and in to whatever extent is necessary according to conditions. At the same time, stamp footholds by raising the feet high and bringing snow from above to compact into a platform that will hold your weight. The softer the snow, the more difficult this is and the more experience, patience, and stamina are required.

At times it is necessary to remove the outer layer of extremely soft snow as you climb in order to get down to something more substantial. A steep trench, perhaps two feet deep, sometimes must be excavated. If the excavation of a deep trench uncovers the disheartening fact that nothing solid lies beneath, the last resort before admitting defeat is to attempt to "swim" up the slope, burying your hands and arms in up to the shoulders, hoping that their greater surface area will make the ascent possible.

Using a Shovel in Place of an Axe

When large amounts of soft snow have to be removed over long stretches, it is better to use a snow shovel instead of the axe. On many Alaskan ridges this has proven a great advantage, and, similarly, many winter climbs are less work if a shovel is employed.

Using the shafts of the ice axe and ice hammer on steep snow. (Photo by John Ruger)

Crampons in Snow Climbing

When snow becomes so hard that steps cannot be kicked, crampons must be donned. The techniques required are covered adequately in the following chapter, dealing with ice climbing technique. The only difference between ice and hard

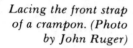

Lacing the front strap of a crampon. (Photo by John Ruger)

snow is that crampons on hard snow are easier to use. Very often if you are wearing crampons in soft snow, you will find them gathering snow, or "balling up," rendering them worse than useless. The most effective method of dealing with this problem is to cut a piece out of a large, heavy-gauge poly bottle that will fit snugly up between the points of your crampons. Anchor the plastic securely with wire laced through holes cut in the material and fastened around the frame of the crampon.

Bivouacs and Snow Caves

In the interest of speed or because there is not enough snow to dig a cave a night in a bivouac sack might be necessary. But when there is snow enough and time enough, dig a snow cave. It is almost always the best thing to do because a cave provides good insulation, is soundproof (important for sleep), and offers protection from even the most violent storms.

Make the entrance to the cave as narrow as you can while allowing yourself room to work. Tunnel far enough back so

A snow cave provides the best form of bivouac protection. (Photo by Jeff Lowe)

that the walls of the cave will have substantial thickness. Make a sleeping shelf above the level of the entrance as this will trap the heat from your body and from cooking. Carve the ceiling into a smooth dome: water will flow down the walls instead of dripping from rugosities. You can close the entrance with packs, a bivouac sack, or snow blocks, but make certain there's adequate ventilation. Punch a few air holes above the entrance with the shaft of your ice axe.

THE BRITTLE TWO-STEP

For years climbers have debated the relative merits of the French and German techniques. The French technique relies on the points of the crampons, which stick down from under the boot, and the German technique (front-pointing) utilizes the two points that protrude from the toe of the boot. With experience, any reasonably unbiased person will see merit in both methods. The techniques described here are a continuum

Left: The object of French technique is to get all ten under-the-boot crampon points into the ice. Right: Using one foot sideways and the front-points of the other on moderate slopes (Pied Troiseme in French). (Photos by John Ruger)

of the two schools: French technique for slopes of from 45 to 60 degrees (depending on the quality of the ice) and front-pointing for steeper slopes.

For those who wish to learn it, French terminology accompanies the illustrations for low and moderate-angled slopes. Over a variety of terrain, an ascent should flow without pause from one technique to another—the climber attacks a steep bulge on front points, then French-steps up the 45-degree slope above. Another goal to set yourself as you learn ice technique is to become capable of using your hand-tools equally well with either hand—to become ambidextrous in their use.

Throughout this chapter it has been convenient to refer to various inclines as "low angle," or "moderate," and so on. The following table is offered as a rough guide to these rather vague terms:

Low angle—up to 45 degrees
Moderate—45 to 60 degrees
Steep—60 to 80 degrees
Extreme—80 to 90 degrees
Overhanging—more than 90 degrees

Another factor that is as important as the angle in deciding on the best technique to use for any given slope is the quality of the ice. Generally speaking, the softer the ice, the more successful you will be using French technique, especially on steeper slopes. On hard, water ice you might start front-pointing at 45 degrees while on neve you might feel confident using *piolet ancre* (French) up to 60 degrees. In effect, then, hard ice makes it seem as though the angle were greater, and a 50-degree gully filled with water ice can be much more demanding than a 65-degree headwall of firm Alpine ice. The main kinds of ice are described below:

Neve—Steps cannot be kicked readily, but crampon points sink in as if the surface were cork. Partially metamorphosed snow on its way to becoming Alpine ice.

Alpine ice—Almost completely metamorphosed snow but still retains some air trapped between the crystals. Varies considerably. The less aerated it is, the more brittle.

Water ice—Frozen water or else the end result of the metamorphosis of snow; it no longer contains air between the crystals.

Step Cutting on Ice

The time-honored art of hewing steps is in danger of being lost as there is seldom a need for it anymore. It's worth learning though, especially for those climbs where only a short stretch of ice will be encountered. Why lug crampons up thousands of feet of rock for one pitch of ice when with a bit of practice you'd be able to carve your way up in twenty minutes? And what happens on a longer climb if you break a crampon? You'll waste a lot of energy trying to learn step-cutting technique on the spot.

There are two basic types of steps: diagonal and pigeonhole. Diagonal steps can be made in either a single or double row (see illustration) while pigeonhole steps ascend straight up the fall line like a ladder, first being used as handholds and then as footholds. A single row of diagonal steps is used on low-angle slopes, and the double row is for moderate inclines when balance is hard to maintain with a single row. Pigeonhole steps are used on steep ice.

Diagonal steps usually are made to accept the whole boot, sideways. Strangely enough, smaller steps can be used if you are not wearing crampons as there is no inner row of points on which to pivot and torque your ankle outward, as is the case with crampons. Cut steps with the adze of your axe, using either the inside or outside hand or both, depending on the length of your axe shaft and the angle of the slope. Examine the slope for any irregularities that might make your cutting job easier.

Begin the step with a chop that will define the boundary of the step closest to you. Each successive chop, moving *away* from your body, should shave a bit more ice. If one series of cuts leaves a step that is too narrow, make another pass, again starting with the cut nearest you and working away. Remove the ice above the step and make room for your ankle with one or two downward chops with the pick. Your steps should slope in slightly, toward the mountain, to lessen the chance of your foot slipping out. At switchbacks, make a step large enough for both feet to assist you in making the transition to a new direction.

Pigeonholes should be spaced about shoulder-width apart and about 18 inches above one another. Face the mountain directly. Make a stop-cut with the adze to define the lower lip of the step. Make all successive cuts above the stop-cut, and you won't fracture out the bottom of the step. Since it is desirable for the step to be deep enough to accept the complete toe-half of your boot, you'll have to deepen it with the pick. The last procedure is to make a good lip at the bottom of the step so that it can be used as a handhold. Small blows with the adze will accomplish this nicely.

Route-Finding on Ice

As on snow, keep an advance eye out for hazards. Once on the climb, be certain not to overlook subtle differences in the consistency or angle of the ice. Slide around that bulge even if it appears not too difficult head-on. A good ice climber conserves his or her strength until it is needed.

Using Crampons

The most important element of good ice climbing technique is positive and confident use of crampons. There is no place for hesitation in their use, and an aggressive approach is best. One way to acquire balance and confidence is to practice on low-angle and moderate slopes with crampons only. Pick an ice flow that is short or else stay near the bottom of a longer slope when practicing with crampons. In this way the need to

To acquire balance and confidence, practice on low-angle slopes with crampons only. (Photo by John Ruger)

rope is avoided and you can concentrate on technique.

To ascend low-angle ice, the ten points under the feet are stamped into the ice. As the ice steepens but remains low-angle, there will come a point when facing the slope and ascending directly will place too great a strain on the ankles as you bend them in an attempt to get all ten points to penetrate the ice. When this point is reached, turn sideways to the slope and ascend diagonally. By pointing your feet sideways you will find it easier to get all ten points into the ice. As you step up, crossing one foot in front of the other, it is natural to lean into the slope slightly, but be aware that this motion might torque the crampon points out of the ice. If you climb with no hands, you will be forced into making the right movements. If you have been making a diagonal ascent to the right and wish to change direction so that you are climbing diagonally to the left, stop with all your weight on the points of your right crampon. Then angle your left foot across the slope in the new direction, bring the right foot around, and commence climbing in the new direction. Reverse the sequence for a right turn.

To descend low-angle ice, face the valley, bend your knees enough so that you can get all ten points into the ice (the steeper the ice, the more bend in the knees), and walk down. Keep your upper body forward, and transfer your weight

This climber practices descending a low-angle slope without an ice axe. (Photo by John Ruger)

completely with each step. Don't sit back—if you do, it is impossible to fully weight the crampon points when you step forward, and they won't bite well. The end result of all this is sort of a deep-knee-bend goosestep, which requires strong thighs.

After you have practiced enough to feel confident on a short stretch of low-angle ice in ascent and descent, pick a slightly steeper slope.

On moderate ice the most efficient technique utilizes the front-points of one crampon and the ten points of the other crampon. Keep the heel of the foot that is front-pointing low, and point the other foot sideways, bending the ankle so that all ten points penetrate the ice. Alternating the role of the feet minimizes fatigue in feet, ankles, and calves. After some practice, you'll find that it is easy to relax and enjoy climbing on moderate slopes using this technique.

It's easiest to come down a moderate slope facing in, front-pointing with both feet. Your body should be away from the ice—weight over the crampons. If your points are sharp, body weight is enough to make them bite. Kicking them in only wastes energy except perhaps on unusually hard ice. When using front-points, be careful not to place them in a way that might cause them to torque out a chunk of ice as you move up or down.

Keep the heels at least this low in relation to the toes when front-pointing. (Photo by John Ruger)

If both points are biting and are in a horizontal plane (point to point) and your heel is low (thus relaxing your calves), you are front-pointing well. Now you're ready for even steeper ice, but you'll probably want an axe.

Using Ice Axe and Crampons

Back to the beginning. Back to the low-angle slope. You've practiced without an axe to get the feeling of balance. Now grab your axe, head in the palm of your hand and pick pointing forward. On low-angle slopes, use it as a cane with the point in the ice. While traversing or ascending diagonally, carry the axe in the uphill hand; if you change direction, change hands. Walk down the slope using the axe as a cane also, angling the head away from the ice to cause the spike to bite well.

When the angle of the slope nears 40 degrees, you'll find that holding the axe across the body (head in the outside hand and the hand closest to the ice holding the shaft near the spike, which is pricked into the ice) offers the best balance. When holding the axe this way, ascend diagonally as you did on the same slope with the crampons only. When changing direction, you'll have to switch the position of the hands on the axe, naturally.

In descent hold the axe across the body in the same manner

The ice axe is used as a cane to descend a low-angle slope (piolet canne in French). (Photo by John Ruger)

but face directly downhill. Greater security can be achieved for descending a short, steeper section by holding the shaft of the axe in one hand, near the spike, and swinging the pick into the ice below you. Use the axe as a bannister—slight outward tension on the shaft will keep the curved pick locked in the ice. Practice is required to be able to plant the pick solidly on the first try. Don't pull up short; let the ice absorb the full force of the swing.

This series of 6 photos shows the ice axe used diagonally across the chest on a moderate slope. The last two photos show how to change direction from right to left. The French name for this technique is piolet ramasse. (Photos by John Ruger)

On moderate ice you learned the relaxed method of climbing the slope directly with the front-points of one crampon and the points under the boot of the other crampon. Add an axe and you have one of the easiest of all methods for climbing ice. Hold the axe diagonally across your body, its head high, and the pick toward the ice. One hand should grasp the shaft low and the fingers of the other hand should curl over the head, with the thumb behind the shaft. Now as you climb punch the pick into the ice with every set of steps

Front-pointing and using the palms down on top of the axe and hammer. This technique is used for moderate slopes of hard ice (piolet panne in French). (Photo by John Ruger)

you take. Be aware of the inner rhythm that guides your movements. When you're in tune with yourself, this technique is pure joy and is the key to many long, Alpine ascents.

The process can be reversed for going back down with the exception that it is simpler to front-point with both feet. If the ice is hard and brittle (water ice) and you feel uneasy with the purchase that punching the pick into the ice gives, you can swing the axe from the handle to make the pick bite as deeply as you wish. This wastes energy, however, and on most Alpine ice is not necessary.

With an ice axe and crampons you can enter the realm of *steep ice* climbing. Though it is possible to climb ice of 60 to 70 degrees without an axe, not many feel confident on such steep slopes relying completely on front-points. So find some steep ice and start front-pointing with both crampons (you'll find it almost impossible to bend your ankles enough to get all the bottom points in with one foot sideways). Also use your axe as recommended for moderate ice. You won't tire as quickly if you keep your heels low. Practice traversing with short sideways steps, crossing one foot over the other when that is comfortable. When descending, keep your buttocks out and the weight directly over the crampons. As in rock climbing, you must not hug the mountain.

On increasingly steep slopes, the pick of the axe can be swung into the ice for greater security. The second photo shows how to maintain balance while replanting the axe (pi-olet ancre in French). (Photo by John Ruger)

Left: This photo shows the piolet ramasse used to descend a moderate slope. Right: Descending a steeper slope (piolet rampe in French). (Photos by John Ruger)

Using Ice Hammer, Ice Axe, and Crampons

The use of an ice hammer along with the axe is not necessary on ice of low or moderate angle. In fact, it might be considered an unhealthy habit to reach for the hammer at the first sign of steepness because you might develop a dependency. It is better to confine yourself to the tools that are truly needed for the job. But when the ice rears up so steeply that balance is hard (or impossible) to maintain when the pick of the axe is removed from the ice or when the ice is so hard and brittle that none of your points seem to be penetrating very deeply, the use of a companion tool is justified. On extreme ice both ice hammer and axe are necessary. With a good tool in each hand and rigid crampons in place, there are few ice pitches that can repulse an experienced and determined climber—even overhanging stretches are not out of the question!

Get the Swing of Things

As was said earlier, the sound of a well-placed tool is a solid "thunk." Any vibration or hollow feeling is reason for suspicion, and a suspect tool must be removed and replaced. There is no future in the assumption that it *probably* will hold. The climber must know, beyond a reasonable doubt, that it *will* hold.

The only way you can develop a good working knowledge of the relative security of any given placement is through practice. Take your hammer and your axe and go to the bottom of the practice flow. Spend some time swinging both into the ice. Examine the ice closely. What happens when you place your tool on a bulge or bump? The ice often will flake

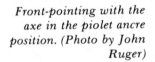

Front-pointing with the axe in the piolet ancre position. (Photo by John Ruger)

off. But try a little hollow; perhaps a small space or hole where two icicles are incompletely welded together. More often than not you'll find your picks sticking well in such a place. Use enough force to get the picks to bite securely but not so much that you have trouble removing them.

If you're using Terrordactyls, you'll need to develop a sharp, downward flick of the wrist at the end of the swing. Often, several short flicks are better than one hard swing with these tools; a little pocket is made that soon offers a secure hole in which the tool can be hooked.

If the tools of your choice have curved picks, then your swing can have a more natural arc. No special swing need be practiced—just accuracy. Choose the spot where you want the pick to penetrate, concentrate on it for a brief moment, and then continue to watch that spot as you swing. Remember, follow through with the swing. Don't pull up short; let the ice absorb the force of the blow. The proper swing for a Hummingbird is something of a compromise: swing normally but with more of an arc from the wrist and only a short windup. *All tools require concentration on the point of impact*; that's of prime importance.

Thick gloves and mittens, such as the Dachstien mitts normally worn by ice climbers, can cause problems in the orientation of the pick during the swing. Their clumsiness and bulk effectively round out the oval cross-section of the shaft. The only remedy for this, short of wearing thin gloves or none at all, is to practice swinging the tools wearing heavy mitts until you can keep the pick oriented in spite of the difficulty. Practice until your arms are like rubber, for on a difficult lead they often will be.

A Note from the Doctor for
Terrordactyl Knuckle or Hummer Bummers

If you have been practicing what has been preached in the last few paragraphs, you will no doubt already have experienced the initial symptoms of one of these recent additions to the vocabularly of human deformity. The problem stems from the tendency to place the tools with their shafts right against the ice and consequently bash your knuckles. Once you've bruised them, you'll be likely to continue the damage until you give them a rest cure. Better than that, however, is prevention. Unfortunately, total prevention is not possible unless you feel like wearing some sort of steel handguard as you climb. But if that makes you feel too much like a knight in shining armor, there is something you can do: learn to use your tools so that the shaft ends up close to the ice but not hard against it upon completion of the swing. It's a more subtle skill than one might first imagine and one well worth perfecting. On low-angle ice leaving the shaft several inches away from the ice makes removal easier, too.

Get a Sling on Things

Slings, or wrist loops, are another often overused item among the ice climber's equipment. They tend to make it too easy to hang from your hand-tools, thus making it possible to climb without proper crampon technique. It is best to do without slings until they are absolutely necessary. However, few climbers are capable of hanging around on long stretches of extremely steep or vertical ice without some sort of attachment to their hammers. So wrist loops are useful, even indispensable, at times and deserve a full discussion.

The best arrangement for slinging an ice axe seems to be something along the lines shown in the photo. The small

Sling your ice axe as shown in the first photo; otherwise it will hang as in the second photo and be harder to re-grasp. (Photos by Jeff Lowe)

diameter cord running from the wrist loop around the shaft of the axe near the bottom is there to keep the axe within easy grasp after letting it go to place a screw or climb a bit of rock. Without this feature the axe will hang as shown in the other photo, and great skill must be developed to flip it up and catch it. As you can see, this small loop should be anchored to the wrist sling and loosely passed around the shaft, making it possible to slide the hand up and down the shaft unimpeded.

It seems a good idea to provide for easy removal of whatever wrist loop arrangement you end up devising. That way you'll be more likely to remove them when they are not needed, and they won't become a crutch. Most normal Alpine ice routes don't require wrist loops nor do many of the easier frozen waterfalls. The axe can be carried in a hammer holster or clipped to your gear sling with a carabiner through the eye in the head.

Be certain to make the loop large enough to accept your hand easily, even while wearing your bulkiest combination of gloves and mittens. You can grab the axe through the loop as you would grasp a ski pole or you can slip your hand straight through, whichever way suits you best. The important thing about the loop on the axe (and all wrist loops, for that matter) is that the length be adjusted properly. For the best swing and to avoid the problem of the spike sticking out too far and tending to dig into the ice as you swing, make certain that the sling is long enough so that your gloved hand grasps the axe right at the ferrule, immediately above the spike.

Attaching the axe to your body with a cord is a practice that might be more confusing than helpful. This cord is extraneous to the use of the axe. An image comes to mind here of Captain Complex, tangled in his cords and lashed to the side of the Great White Icicle.

A good sling can be made for the Alpine hammer by draping a piece of webbing over the head, crossing it in front of the shaft, completing the loop behind the shaft, and finally taping it securely in place with any good strapping tape. This avoids the need to drill a hole in the handle. A smooth profile is formed, especially if the loop is sewn instead of tied. A sewn loop is a good idea if you hope to be able to remove the hammer from most hammer holsters.

The Alpine hammer often is used as a third tool in conjunction with an axe and a North Wall hammer on extreme ice; it is very handy for placing and removing screws and pitons. During this process it is often convenient to release it from your grasp to fiddle with carabiners, etc., so it is the only ice tool that it really makes sense to have attached to the body. But the common method of attaching the hammer cord to a loop that is draped across one shoulder and under the other arm creates a potential hazard. Conceivably, you could hang yourself if you slipped and lost your grip when the pick was firmly imbedded in the ice. An alternative is to tie the cord from the hammer directly into the waist loop of your swami belt or harness.

CLIMBING STEEP ICE

With any combination of two tools (an axe and a hammer, two axes, two hammers, or an axe and a North Wall hammer), you're ready to begin front-pointing on steep and extreme ice. Now take your tools to the practice area and *find some steep ice*.

Look the ice over carefully, find a likely spot, and plant your first tool. Don't reach too high. Then plant your second tool, far enough away from the first tool so that you don't fracture out a block of ice between the two. Relying on the tools just enough for balance, stand up on one crampon and then the other. If the ice is hard and smooth, you will have to kick your front-points in. More often than you might imagine, however, it is possible simply to stand with your crampons on a roughness in the slope, and this is a good energy-saving habit to acquire. Look for those bumps and hollows—those cracks and crannies—and treat them as the aid that they are. Such subtle intimacy with the slope is the mark of a good ice climber.

Climb a few feet, moving only one point of contact at a time. Don't let your feet twist out of horizontal alignment as you reach to make a new step. That will cause the front-points to torque in the ice as you stand up, with the possible result of breaking them out. For the same reason, don't let the heel of the lower foot rise as you step up.

Swing, swing. Step, step. Once again you must remember to stand in balance, buttocks away from the ice, weight over the crampons, heels low, and calves relaxed. Relax your vise-like grip on the hand-tools, and let the wrist loops do the work. Make a few sideways steps, conscious of the attitude of your front-points as you kick them in, and take short steps. Make short reaches with the hand-tools. Reverse the traverse. Get used to both directions. And always remember to breathe and relax. Never go so high during practice that you would get hurt if you were to fall.

Now go down. Don't choke up on the shafts of your tools. Just reach down a moderate distance and swing from the wrist more than you normally would. (Terrordactyls seem to work a little better for this.) Step down a short distance, not so far that you leave yourself hanging at full-stretch from your tools. Don't hurry. Never make a move until you are certain that whatever point (or points) you have just planted are secure. Practice on steep ice until it seems easy (it *is*). Don't push yourself to the point of falling off; even from a few feet up it's easy to break an ankle or puncture yourself. Never plant an axe directly in front of your face if you want to avoid losing an eye when it pops out unexpectedly.

After you have *mastered* steep ice, you can begin to consider that bit of vertical stuff you've been eyeing all this time, that is, if you've had the patience to refrain from attempting it already. The extreme ice is what everyone is after, the spectacular stuff that looks so impressive in the photos. Many people are capable of climbing extreme ice their first day out. But that doesn't mean they should. It's better to develop an understanding of the medium and competence on the easier angles first. But when you're ready, you're ready, and only you know when that is.

Back to your perfect practice area, the one with ideal sections of ice of all angles. (It is more likely that by now you will have had to visit several areas to practice all the skills that have been discussed.) Pick a stretch of ice that is laid back slightly from the vertical. Climb on it as you climbed on steep ice. If you really have put in the practice on steep ice, you'll have no trouble here. Treat your axe and hammer (or whatever combination of tools you are using) as portable belays. Never make a move until you are certain they will not pull out even if to do so requires numerous planting tries, which is sometimes the case in very brittle ice. Practice. Practice until you've developed control of mind and muscles. Falls are *not* acceptable. They are too dangerous. The ability to downclimb is as important as the ability to ascend. In a tight situation remember that deep breathing clears the mind and relaxes the muscles.

The Monkey Hang

There is a point in climbing ice that is closer and closer to vertical where it becomes easier to rely heavily on your handtools rather than to try and stay in balance over your frontpoint. Of course, on absolutely vertical or slightly overhanging ice you *must* hang from your hands. In this context, Patey's question, "Apes or Ballerinas?"[2] is easily answered: ice climbing is definitely the "Planet of the Apes." So, climber see, climber do—the "Monkey Hang" was made for you.

Watch Herman, the ice-climbing monkey, who is on the vertical section of the pitch. Thoughtlessly but correctly he hangs straight-armed from his tools, his fanny away from the ice and his feet quite high up under his hands so that his legs form a crooked "L" with his body. In this position the points of his crampons are forced into the ice. Herman then carefully loosens one of his tools but does not completely remove it from the ice (he leaves it loosely hooked). Then he pulls his body into an upright position.

---

2. *Mountain*, May, 1969.

The author uses the monkey hang on the first pitch of The Fang in Utah. (Photo by Wes Kraus)

Practice the monkey hang on less than vertical ice to master the sequence; then try it on a vertical wall. (Photo by John Ruger)

Holding himself with one arm cocked and as much weight as possible on the front-points of his crampons, Herman then removes the tool he already has loosened and reaches high, takes aim, and replaces it. As soon as he is satisfied that the new placement is secure, Herman again hangs straight-armed from it, thus taking the strain of supporting his weight off the cocked arm and transferring it to the skeleton of the straight arm.

Next Herman (who is obviously no dumb monkey) loosens the other tool, stands up, and replaces it above the one he is hanging from, immediately letting his weight hang straight-armed from this new placement. Herman rests for a moment in this position before bringing his feet up closer to his hands to assume the modified "L" position again, ready to repeat the entire process. If you've ever watched the monkeys hanging from the wire of their cages at the zoo, you'll immediately recognize the origin of Herman's technique.

The Monkey Hang is a technique that takes maximum advantage of skeletal strengths by limiting the length of time you must hold yourself up by your arm muscles. An added advantage of this technique is that it allows better purchase for the crampons since they are pushed *into* the ice rather than having a straight sheer-force applied to them, at least while the climber is "resting" in the modified "L" position. The whole technique belongs to the "exterior" style of climbing. Its closest parallel is crack climbing on rock, and it is the ultimate technique in the ice climbing progression, suitable for even overhanging ice if the climber is strong enough, skilled enough, and bold enough. At this point the limits of the possible are different for each individual.

Stemming

The surfaces of most waterfalls really aren't flat but made up of a series of groves, flutes, chimneys, and so forth. Whenever possible, it is good to stem with the feet between these formations. In this way it often is possible to take the weight completely off the arms.

This climber is ascending in the confines of the ice-filled chimney of The Skylight in Colorado. (Photo by Jeff Lowe)

Aiding on Ice

There is an argument that claims all ice climbing is aided since it is apparently impossible without the use of tools. And, therefore, one style of ice climbing is as good as another. Logically speaking, this line of reasoning is irrefutable. But there are those who love climbing for its illogical nature and who feel that *reason* does not explain the rewarding feelings they get when they limit themselves to the least amount of gear and hardware with whicp they can get by. For them the end does not justify the means. The end, in fact, might be next to meaningless. The important consideration is the *quality of the effort*—how one reaches the goal, not the goal itself. There are few ice climbs where equipment beyond two hand-tools, a pair of crampons, and a skillful climber are necessary. But if you must, there are a couple of easy techniques that complicate steep ice climbing (making it very slow as well) but *do* make it easier if less of a commitment.

The most obvious technique for aiding on ice is simply to insert ice screws or pitons at short intervals and clip aid slings into them, exactly as you would on rock. Slightly faster, and quite ingenious, is a technique that was developed in Canada to assist in pioneering efforts on the big frozen waterfalls found there in winter. The climber attaches aid slings to the holes in the spikes of two Terrodactyls. He first places one tool, stands in the aid sling (perhaps also taking some support from the front-points of his crampon), and then places the other tool, making headway in this manner. Though this technique is indeed easier than front-pointing, it has the disadvantage of placing yet another item of gear between the climber and his experience of the ice.

SPECIAL PROBLEMS

Up to this point all the techniques described have assumed continuous ice and good conditions. But what happens when, as is often the case, the ice is thin, rotten, or mixed with rock? Must you go home and come back when conditions are better?

The author using natural handholds on Stewart Falls, Utah. (Photo by Mike Lowe)

Perhaps. But there are many times when thin or rotten ice should not deter you. And mixed climbing, with one foot on ice and the other on rock, is considered by many climbers the finest of all experiences. Techniques to deal with these conditions have been developed. Perhaps "techniques" is the wrong word. It might be better to say that climbers have learned to cope with such diverse conditions and to improvise solutions as needs arose. Such an ability is rare but necessary if you are to have a satisfying experience with your ice climbing. It is the nature of ability that it cannot be *taught*; one person cannot pass his ability on to another. The ability to cope with a large variety of conditions is no exception. But a few hints can be given that might help as you *develop* your own ability.

Thin Ice

On thin ice of moderate angle it often is helpful to use two hand-tools even if the angle is such that you normally would use only one. Sometimes the front-points of your crampons or the picks of your tools can be hooked through the ice and

Climbing thin ice over rock requires delicate movement above all else. (Photo by Jeff Lowe)

onto a hold in the underlying rock. Avoid sudden or sloppy movements that could break the ice. Excessive kicking of feet or slamming of tools is bad for the same reason and will not increase your security. Precision use of what little ice there is, is the ticket.

Rotten Ice

If it is of substantial thickness, rotten ice can be climbed with two ice axes. The extra length of the picks allows greater depth of penetration and thus increases security. On thin and rotten ice take special care to avoid outward pulls on your tools. Even as you raise your body, you should be *pushing down* on the wrist loops, keeping the shafts or handles of the tools close to the ice.

Cauliflower Ice

This is waterfall ice that looks like its namesake or sometimes more like a pine cone standing on its base. Often, it is extremely difficult to get a secure anchorage with the picks of your tools under these conditions. It's better to put your tools away and climb using natural holds. If your wool mitts or gloves are slightly damp, you'll find that they tend to stick quite well to the holds. Using whatever holds the ice has to offer is always an enjoyable way to climb, even when it is not strictly necessary. It's good preparation for those times when conditions dictate the use of natural formations.

Mixed Ice and Rock

Climbing in mixed media is an exercise in imagination. With all the possible configurations of rock, all the variabilities of ice, and the hardware that has been developed for both media, the possible ways to ascend are nearly infinite. Perhaps there is a bit of ice at the back of a steep dihedral, and the dihedral is capped by a small overhang with a thick set of ice crooping

A cone of "cauliflower" ice. The arrow points to a climber on The Rigid Designator in Colorado. (Photo by Jeff Lowe)

Mike Weis climbs on mixed ground on the Eastern Spur of Mount Resplendent in the Canadian Rockies. (Photo by Jeff Lowe)

from its lip. You climb to the overhang, placing your axe and hammer in the ice at the corner of the dihedral and stemming between tiny rock holds on either wall with the front-points of your crampons. Then, after putting your hammer in its holster, with one hand using a crack under the roof as an undercling, you knock a hole in the sheet of ice, lean out, plant your axe securely above the roof, and reach up with the other hand to jam it into a space between two pillars of ice. Finally, you pull yourself up. The possibilities are staggering. The only definite advice that can be given is that the front-points of crampons are almost always better on rock holds than trying to edge using the points underneath the boots. It is a good idea to practice climbing on dry rock to find out what the limits of cramponed climbing really are.

Bouldering without hand-tools puts the climber "in touch" with the ice in more than just a physical way. (Photo by Jeff Lowe)

Snow-Covered Rock

This problem often is dealt with more effectively wearing crampons than Vibram soles. Climbing with crampons on rock is a study in the precision use of holds, and it takes a lot of practice to become accustomed to it. You'll amaze yourself at how small nicks in the rock give a good purchase for a front-point or two.

THWARTING GRAVITY'S EVIL EFFORTS

I can't give a reason why / I should ever want to die.

—Commander Cody

With a rope from above, any reasonably adept climber will have little trouble with most ice pitches. The difficulty comes on the lead, when you must stop on a vertical step that is too long to climb unprotected, and somehow you must hang by one hand and place a piton or screw with the other. The technique described on the following pages will be of some help, but there is nothing more important than being in good physical condition.

Double Ropes

The use of double ropes on very steep and technical ascents is strongly recommended, although it is not necessary for reducing friction of rope against ice. The rope almost always runs easily anyway across the slippery surface. Even the most careful climber might at one time or another become stranded on a pitch, perhaps because the belayer pulled up a loop of slack just at the moment the climber was planting an axe, the result being a neatly sliced in two rope. A double 9 mm rope will at least provide a second chance. Fancy double rope techniques are not really needed, again because of the low friction qualities of the ice medium. Just clip both ropes through whatever protection you place.

"Waterproof" Ropes

In conditions where the rope gets wet and then freezes, the rope might become as stiff as a cable and refuse to run through carabiners or be manipulated into knots. This situation can make advance or retreat nearly impossible. Thankfully, many rope manufacturers have come out with water repellent ropes (sometimes referred to as "waterproof"). They greatly reduce the chance of being stranded. For ice climbing, the additional cost is worth it.

Three Hand-Tools

From personal experience, the author can attest to the unreliability of the picks on most ice axes and hammers. The latest claims of the manufacturers notwithstanding, picks still break sometimes, usually when the ice is extremely cold and brittle and often when the climber is *"in extremis."* The solution to this problem is to bring along a third tool whenever the ice is steep and there is a chance that a pick might break.

Ice Axe Belay

There are several methods of ice axe belaying, which will be listed below. But it is much better to be prepared for snow belays by including a deadman in your climbing gear; the security of even the best ice axe belay is minimal.

1) The simplest belay is achieved by driving the shaft of the axe into the snow at an acute angle upward toward the slope and then tying a sling around the shaft at snow-level to tie into. Enough slack should be allowed in the belayer's tie-in so that he may station himself well below the axe, thus eliminating any outward force that could tend to dislodge it.

2) The boot-axe belay is achieved by stamping out a platform in the snow, driving the shaft of the axe in deeply at the rear of the platform, placing the uphill foot firmly in front of the axe, and passing the rope from the climber over the toe of

the boot, around the shaft, and then across the instep of the boot. The belayer must hold the head of the axe solidly with his uphill hand. Braking is achieved by bending the rope back across the instep of the boot with the lower hand.

3) The ice axe may also be used as a deadman, although without the same effectiveness as an aluminum plate. Tie a prusik around the middle of the shaft. Cut a slot crossways to the slope and large enough to accept the axe. Cut another at right angles to the first slot to allow the prusik sling to run downhill to the belayer. Packing snow into the slots after placing the axe will somewhat strengthen this belay.

Bollards

A bollard is a hand-hewn mushroom of snow or ice around which the climbing rope is looped to form a belay. A well-made bollard is very secure, and its use allows many Alpine ascents to be accomplished with a minimum of gear—very satisfying and practical when a climb has a long approach hike.

An ice bollard. (Photo by Jeff Lowe)

In soft snow a bollard must sometimes have a diameter of as much as ten feet. The required size diminishes as conditions get solider until only eighteen inches or two feet are required in cohesive, hard ice. In softer snow it is sometimes helpful to line the back groove with clothing or other articles to help spread the load over a larger surface area.

The bollard should have a half-moon shape, opening downhill and with elongated points. The smoother the arc, the more evenly the load will be distributed. The arc might have to be as deep as eighteen inches or so at the back (in soft snow), or it might only need six inches or less in good ice. The groove should slope down at the back and in at the sides, forming a lip to keep the rope in place. The groove should be deepest at the rear and gradually become shallower toward the points of the half-moon.

When chopping a bollard out of ice, take care to avoid causing fracture lines that might undermine it. Using light blows with the adze, cut the outline of the smallest dimension the bollard will be (this would be called a stop-cut in woodworking), and then work away from the outline. The pick of a Hummingbird works fantastically well for forming the final groove for the rope; using the pick of an axe is a little harder.

Since bollards can hold a force only in one direction, it might be necessary to cut one for an upward pull as well as one for downward resistance and to tie them together for a non-directional anchor.

The Deadman

The deadman has raised the quality of snow belays from the "imaginary" category to something more substantial. Tests have been conducted that indicate that a well-placed deadman in solid snow will offer about 1,600 pounds of resistance to a downward pull, and it will continue to offer this resistance as it "flukes" deeper into the snow. A slot must be cut to accept the cable or sling, and the deadman is placed about a 45-

degree angle to the slope. If the cable slot is not deep enough, there is a risk of the deadman being pulled up out of the snow. Similarly, if the deadman is placed at too shallow an angle, it also will pop out. The deadman, like the bollard, is a one-direction anchor. In soft snow some extra security can be achieved by first packing a large area and then placing the deadman in it.

Placing Snow Pickets

Drive pickets in as you would tent stakes, at an angle to the anticipated direction of pull. Any picket not fully driven should be tied off at snow-level to reduce leverage.

Natural Protection

Occasionally on an Alpine ice route, and often on a frozen waterfall, the ice will have a configuration that can be used for belay or protection. Taking advantage of these formations is a rewarding and energy-saving activity. A runner can be passed around a large pillar of ice for a solid belay, or rock-climbing chocks can be used in slots on the surface of the ice. Use your imagination and don't overlook the obvious.

Placing Ice Screws and Pitons

Ice screws offer the most secure form of anchor for protection or belay. The method of placement depends on the type of ice and the angle. Most Alpine ice has a relatively insubstantial surface layer that should be removed with the adze of the axe before inserting the screw. If the ice is extremely rotten, a large step should be cut in the slope and the screw placed vertically downward at the back. In addition, snow packed around the head and eye will slow the melt-out tendency in warm ice or when the sun shines on the screw. If the surface ice is good, the screw may be placed at a slight acute upward angle right at the surface. Regardless of the quality of the ice,

Left: This climber places an ice screw on nearly vertical ice while hanging from the wrist loop of his axe. Right: Inserting your arm through the wrist loop to the elbow allows you to hold the screw during placement.

the screw will go in much easier if a deep starting hole is made first with the pick of one of your tools. The hole should be about the diameter of the screw, minus the threads. The most common error is to make the hole too large and not deep enough.

On low to steeply angled slopes it often is useful to chop a step to stand in before attempting to insert a screw. When the ice is extremely steep or vertical, the little added security gained by chopping a step is negated by the extra time and effort required to do so. On such ice you must hang by the wrist loop of one tool (with either your hand or elbow—see illustration) while you place the screw with the other hand (this is where a good starting hole is important). Or you can opt for the easier method of hanging on a sling connected from one of your hand-tools to your harness, thus freeing both hands for the work. This method seems too much like aid to be satisfactory, though it is widely practiced.

On any sort of ice at any angle, you must make a good starting hole and then begin turning the screw by hand. Once the threads have begun to grip really well, you may use the pick of a tool or another screw or piton for extra leverage to turn it the remainder of the way. A modified ratchet, as described earlier, makes the job much easier. Avoid putting sideways torque on the pick of any ice tool while placing a screw as picks are weak in that direction. *Never* use the pick of a Hummingbird to drive a screw unless you want your bird to shed its beak unexpectedly.

Drivable ice pitons such as the Salewa spiral-piton and the LAS tubular piton make leading a steep pitch easier because they can be placed much more easily than screws. A good starting hole still is required for one-hand placement. Many small taps are better than a few heavy blows because they help the piton melt its way into the ice rather than fracture it so badly that it can't be trusted. The brittler the ice, the gentler must be the taps.

Try to place screws and pitons in natural depressions in the ice; by so doing, you will observe that few of the fracture lines made by the insertion of the screw or piton will travel to the surface. (The opposite effect can be seen on bulges.)

Setting Up a Normal Belay with Ice Screws

Only ten feet of rope left? And you're on a slope of good ice? Well stop, chop a step, and stand in it. Now clear the bad ice from the surface or cut a step, if necessary, to get down to good ice at about shoulder-level and place a screw. Tie into it with a clove hitch or figure-of-eight knot, and inform your second that you are off belay so that he may begin removing one of his anchors, thus saving some time.

Next place a second screw, two feet or more *above* the first. The upper screw will be handy as the first running belay on the next pitch. Tie the climbing rope into the second screw

To belay, chop a step to stand in; place two or more screws; and tie into them with clove hitches. The final photo in this series shows the ice axe used as a back-up for the belay. If the climber clips into the carabiner he is holding with his left hand, he will equalize the force on both screws. (Photos by John Ruger)

with a clove hitch, and take up the slack between the screws so that the second screw will act as a backup in the event the first screw should begin to fail. Now widen and deepen your step to form a good stance for the belay, after which it is not a bad idea to plant your axe securely in the ice away from the screws but close enough to clip it into the belay set-up with the wrist loop or a runner. Never place screws so closely together that fracture lines radiating from one might connect with those radiating from the other. (Usually, two feet apart is sufficient.) Also be careful not to disturb the ice around screws with your crampons or other tools. In rotten ice use more screws.

Setting Up a Hanging Belay

Very rarely (only on the most severe climbs), there is no break in the extreme angle of the ice for more than a full rope length. But if the ice is of good quality, a secure hanging belay can be arranged, especially if the air temperature is well

Looking down from a hanging belay. Note the natural protection achieved by passing a runner around an icicle above the climber. (Photo by Mike Kennedy)

below freezing, in which case the screws will not have a tendency to melt out from the pressure of your body weight.

Three screws connected in series with clove hitches to take up the slack between them provide an adequate belay on good ice. Once you have inserted the first screw, hang from it in your belay seat or harness, but it might be advisable to wait until you are attached to a second screw also before giving the off-belay signal to your partner. After placing a third screw, you might wish to pass the rope to your second through a carabiner at the screw before bringing him up.

Protecting Thin Ice

Perhaps, in the interest of safety, it might be better to give up a climb when ice is very thin. However, if you insist on pushing it, there are a few tricks that might net you some halfway decent protection. If the ice is thin but well bonded to the underlying rock, you can insert a screw or two as far as possible and tie off their shafts with short runners next to the ice to reduce the leverage.

If the ice is separated from the underlying rock by an inch or more, two other methods of protection are feasible. You simply can punch two holes in the ice, some distance apart, and thread a long runner through one and out the other. Or you can make a vertical slot in the ice about an inch wide and as long as a screw; then tie a runner around the middle of a screw, insert the screw vertically through the slot, and turn it sideways behind the ice sheet, making a sort of deadman.

Moving Simultaneously on Alpine Ascents

"Protection" on some Alpine ice routes is synonymous with speed. If you take too many belays or place too many intermediate screws, you might find that you have "protected" yourself into an afternoon full of rockfall or avalanche. A compromise method between belaying every pitch and climbing

The author climbing mixed snow, ice, and rock on Cascade Falls, Colorado.
(Photo by Mike Gilbert)

unroped is for the climbers to move simultaneously, roped together and with one or more screws between them. Every so often it is necessary for the lead person to stop and take a proper belay, bringing the second up (who will by now have all the screws). This is a fine opportunity to change leaders, which from a psychological standpoint might be desirable. This method can be employed safely only when the angle of the slope and condition of the ice are such that both climbers feel very secure and that the rope is almost an unnecessary amenity anyway.

4

The Hardwater Guide

Climbing guides are notorious for leading people astray. I remember doing a route in the Tetons, Sentinel Turret, years ago, with my brother Mike. We were certain we had found the start of the climb according to the book, and confidently attacked. Immediately, we were lost and spent the rest of the day trying (and often succeeding) to force the features of the rock to fit those described in the guide. We never completed the climb but ended up on a little tower staring at an absolutely blank summit wall. Since then I have learned to use a guide properly, that is, not as an excuse to ignore the route during the approach but as a complement to observations made from a distance. A guide is no free ride. You've got to put *yourself* in the driver's seat.

RATE YOUR TURN

In North America there has never been a grading system for ice that is both flexible enough to be widely applicable and precise enough to be truly informative. Many climbers see this state of confusion as beneficial to maintaining the character of the ice experience since anything that is too well defined automatically loses some of its mystery. However, ice climbing has had such a great amount of publicity recently that the mystery is nearly gone anyway. It seems a good time to introduce a complete and concise grading system that can be used throughout the continent. The following grading system has been worked out over a period of several years. Only time will tell if it will serve the needs of ice climbers.

Rather than starting from scratch in designing a rating system for ice, it is desirable to incorporate and expand the existing systems: the Yosemite Decimal System for rock and the Scottish grading for ice. The composite system thus formed is good for two reasons: 1) A great many people are familiar with the YDS, and quite a few understand the Scottish grades. Therefore, these two systems, when adapted, can be made into something that many climbers should be able to understand quickly. 2) The composite grading system thus formed can be used to describe *any* climb, including pure rock routes, pure ice routes, and mixed routes. Furthermore, it does not require alteration of the descriptions of rock routes that are already rated by the YDS.

Briefly, the Yosemite Decimal System rates a climb in three parts:* 1) An overall grade designated by Roman numerals I-VI; 2) the hardest free climbing move, with 5.0 representing the easiest and 5.12 currently the most difficult; and 3) the hardest aid moves (if any), which are designated with a capital A (for aid) followed by a number from 1 to 5. Thus, the rating for a rock climb might read like this: "The Naked Edge [name

---

*For a complete explanation of the YDS, see *A Climber's Guide to Yosemite Valley* by Steve Roper.

of climb], IV, 5.11," which means it is a moderate length climb (IV) of great free climbing difficulty (5.11), with no aid. Now let's take a look at the Scottish grading for ice.

The Scottish grades of I to V originally were intended to convey the overall difficulty and seriousness of a climb in much the same way as the YDS overall grade. However, over the years the grades have come to have *two* meanings: one is an indication of overall difficulty and the other, an indication of technical, or individual move, difficulty. Thus, a climber might say that a certain climb, because of its lack of length, is only a IV but has moves of grade V. The Scottish system has been copied in New England. The New England Ice Grades have some rough similarities to the Scottish grades as do those in use in the Canadian Rockies (where a grade VI has been added because of the length of some of the winter climbs).

If we decide to combine the Scottish system and the YDS without change or adaptation, we see that they overlap in the overall grade area. But if we keep the YDS overall category and use only the newer, i.e., *technical*, meaning of the Scottish grade, these two values can be used in defining a popular climb such as the Black Ice Couloir on the Grand Teton. Thus, "Black Ice Couloir, YDS IV, Scottish III." Or, more concisely: "Black Ice Couloir, IV, S3."

We can do even more with the Scottish grade if we give it two categories and instead of an "S" before the grade, use "AI" (for Alpine Ice) or "WI" (for Water Ice). This informs the reader of the kind of climb he is contemplating, seasonal or permanent ice. The Black Ice Couloir rated this way would be "IV, AI3." Furthermore, if the climb also has pure rock climbing difficulties, as does the Black Ice Couloir, it is an easy matter to so indicate: "Black Ice Couloir, IV, AI3, 5.6." If there were aid involved in the climb, we easily could have added that rating also.

In the example the ice comes before the rock for a reason: in the Black Ice Couloir much more ice is encountered by the climber than the rock, and so the rating gives it a more prominent position. If rock difficulties predominate, we would

Name of Climb	Length	Overall	Hardest Rock/ Ice or Both[1]	Aid (if any)
West Rib, Mt. McKinley	3,000 m	V	AI2	
Keystone Green Steps	175 m	IV-V	WI5	
Central Couloir, Mt. Kitchener	1,100 m	V	AI5, 5.9	
Cascade Gully, Bluff	100 m	II	WI3	
Polar Circus	500 m	VI	WI5	
Skyladder, Mt. Andromada	500 m	II	AI2	
North Face, Mt. Athakasca	400 m	III	AI3	
Repentance, Cathedral Ledge	130 m	III	WI5	
Black Dike, Cannon Mt.	175 m	III-IV	WI5	
Black Ice Couloir	600 m	IV	AI3, 5.6	
Northwest Couloir, Middle Teton	300 m	II	AI3	
Bridalveil Falls	120 m	IV	WI5+-6 (see below)[2]	
Stairway to Heaven, Utah	250 m	III	WI5	
Widow's Tears, Yosemite	300 m	V	WI5	
V-Notch, Pallisades	275 m	III	WI3	
Liberty Ridge, Mt. Rainier	1,300 m	IV	AI2	
Willis Wall, Damocles Rib, Mt. Rainier	1,200 m	V	AI3	

---

1. In order of predominance.
2. Another grade must be added to the technical ice category if the system is not to become top heavy with an overbundance of climbs in the WI5 grade.

see something like this: "North Rib of Mount Temple (Canadian Rockies) V, 5.7, AI5." The ice grading alone will suffice whenever the nature of the climbing is so "mixed" that crampons are worn at all times, even though short sections of pure rock are encountered.

In the author's opinion the *length* (vertical relief), which will be given in meters, is one more bit of information that will be useful in giving an idea of just how *concentrated* the difficulties are on any given climb. The length when compared with the overall grade gives an indication of the relative concentration of difficulties. The Black Ice Couloir and Bridalveil Falls are both grade IV climbs, but the former is 600 meters long and the latter only 120 meters. On Bridalveil the difficulties must be concentrated indeed to make up for its lack of length.

The list on page 123 of popular or well-known climbs has been compiled to illustrate this system.

And now, with all of this discussion about ratings behind us, we can go on to the guide.

ALASKA

Ahh! Alaska! For the ice climber Alaska has everything. From the long glacial and snow slog of the West Buttress of *Denali* (McKinley) to huge ice faces such as the north faces of Deborah and Hunter to incredible gully climbs in the Cathedral Spires to big winter falls around Valdez, the Portage Glacier, Juneau, and on and on. Alaska is an ice-climbing paradise. Like everything in Alaska, the ice climbing there is on a grand scale. In terms of the amount of climbing and the size and quality of the climbs, Alaska is second to none. Its potential has scarcely been scratched. In fact, it is possible that somewhere within this huge state lies the *ultimate* ice climb, which might turn out to be a runnel of water on the East Face of the Moose's Tooth frozen into a grand cataract by the cold of winter. Or perhaps one of the big faces on the high peaks of McKinley, Foraker, or Saint Elias has a secret that is yet undiscovered. At least one thing is certain: Alaska ice climbing is on a par with that anywhere in the world.

But why is there so much ice in Alaska? The answer is easy: weather, latitude, and altitude. The combination of these three elements insures plenty of precipitation, that this precipitation often will come in the form of snow, and that the snow will have plenty of opportunity between the time it falls and when it finally melts to metamorphose into various sorts of Alpine ice. The long summer days also provide the heat necessary for metamorphosis. The extremes of climatic conditions found in Alaska are reflected in the extremes found in its ice forms. All the snow that has been melted by the summer sun runs down the cliff faces, gullies, and hillsides. Winter then creates vast amounts of water ice upon which the climber of frozen waterfalls may ply his craft.

But the very reasons why there is so much ice in Alaska are cause for caution on the climber's part. On a big face a heavy storm might trap the unlucky for several days or a week. A cornice might collapse in the heat in the summer sun and scour the gully at the very time you have chosen to ascend it. An unexpected bivouac on a frozen waterfall occasioned by a five-hour December day might make frostbite the companion of an unprepared climber. The point is that Alaska not only has some of the greatest ice climbs in the world but also some of the most prominent objective hazards. The size and beauty of the climbs is equalled by the dangers inherent in them. Alaska is a good place for climbers with years of experience behind them.

One peculiar characteristic of much of the climbing in Alaska is its remoteness. This remoteness means that usually the likelihood of rescue is slim and that any climbing you are likely to do will require more than a day or two. Often it is necessary to fly in to the best areas or at least use dog teams or horses. That, of course, has the aesthetic advantage of maintaining the "Alaskan flavor" of the trip.

There are no guidebooks available to the ranges of Alaska except for a small "Map-guide" to a few routes on McKinley, which is published by the Alaska Alpine Company, P.O. Box 1044, Anchorage, Alaska 99510. Current and back issues of the *American Alpine Journal* (which is available in many mountaineering supply stores or from the American Alpine Club, 113 East 90th Street, New York, NY 10028) are the best sources of information on routes that have been climbed. Research into possixle new routes will be assisted by a letter to Bradford Washburn, Curator of the Boston Museum of Natural Science. Washburn is *the* knowledgeable authority on the remaining possibilities in Alaska. Even more, he has a huge catalog of extremely high quality black and white photographs of almost any area you can name. These photos are available for a remarkably low price.

Beyond the *Alpine Journal* and Bradford Washburn, it is possible to discover information in the form of articles and expeditionary notes in the pages of the magazines *Climbing, Mountain,* and *Summit,* all of which are available at many mountain shops.

In Anchorage the people at Alaska Mountaineering and Hiking (AMH) can give you up-to-date information on many new climbs and also might point you in the direction of some good and reasonably accessible ice climbing along the Portage Glacier in the winter and in the Chugach Mountains in the summer.

Beginning with the Alaska range (in the middle of the state) and working south, the list that follows is a spotty and very incomplete attempt to suggest some of the finer ice routes that have been done. It is worth nothing once more, however, that the routes that have been done so far are merely the tip of the iceberg.

Alaska Range

Routes on Mt. McKinley:
1) Direct South Face, 2,500 m, VI, AI3-4
    a) British Direct Variation, 3,000 m. VI, AI3-4
2) Wickersham Wall (Canadian), 3,000 m, VI, AI2-3

    b) Wickersham Wall (Harvard), 3,500 m, VI,
3) West Rib of South Face, 3,000 m, VI, AI3
4) Cassin Ridge, 3,000 m, VI, AI4, 5.7

Routes on Foraker:
1) Archangel (north) Ridge, 3,000 m, VI, AI3
2) French (S.SE.) Ridge, 3,000 m, VI (VII?), AI4-5
3) South Ridge (American, 1968), 3,000 m, VI, AI4
4) Mount Russel, original, 1,500 m, V, AI3-4

Mt. Hunter:
1) West Ridge, 2,700 m (vertically) 4 hor. miles,
    V, AI3
2) Northwest Spur (1977), 2,300 m, AI5
3) Northeast Ridge, 1,700 m, V, AI4
4) Northeast Face, 1,700 m, V, AI4

Mt. Huntington:
1) French (west) Ridge, 1,500 m, V, AI4
2) Northeast Ridge, 1,700 m, VI, AI4-5

Mt. Deborah:
1) Original (Becky, Meybohm, Harrer) Route,
    2,000 m, V, AI4
2) Northwest Ridge (1977), 2,000 m, V, AI4
3) North Face, 2,000 m, VI, AI5

Chugach Mountains:
1) Bridalveil Falls (near Valdez), 200 m, IV, WI5
2) Keystone Green Steps (also near Valdez),
    175 m, V, WI5

St. Elias Mountains:
1) East Ridge, 3,000 m, VI, AI4

Mt. Logan (included with Alaska for geographical continuity
although Logan lies in Canada):
1) Hummingbird Ridge, 4,000 m, VI (VII?), AI4

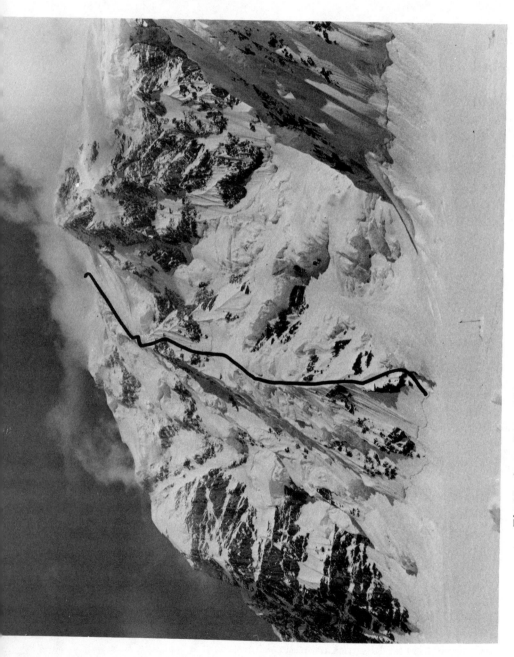

The Northwest Spur of Mount Hunter, Alaska. (Photo by Jeff Lowe)

TWO ALASKAN CLIMBS

The Northwest Spur, Mount Hunter

Grade: 2,300 m, VI, AI5.

Comments: The Northwest Spur is a regular magical mystery tour, with all sorts of fine problems from snow aretes to cornices to ice cliffs to mixed climbing on the "Triangle."

Season: May-July or August.

Location: Rises out of Southeast Fork, Kahiltna Glacier (normal landing site for west and south side McKinley climbs), Alaska Range.

Approach: Fly from Talkeetna, 50 miles distant, or drive to Petersville at the base of the Kahiltna Glacier and ski or snowshoe up the glacier for 5 or 6 days to reach the Southeast Fork. Flying time is ½ hour! Contact Talkeetna Air Taxi or Cliff Hudson for flight arrangements.

Route Description: Cross the bergschrund to the left of the toe of the spur (this minimizes exposure to ice cliffs that hang on the right side of the spur). After 300 or 400 feet, skirt a rock band by way of a short gully on the right. Then angle back up and left until the crest of the spur is met. Follow this until

On the Triangular Face, the Northwest Spur of Mount Hunter. (Photo by Jeff Lowe)

a serac-like obstacle is met about the 450-meter level. A pitch or two of steep climbing on the right side of this leads to easier cruising for 300 meters up a trough between seracs on the crest of the spur, which is now quite broad and ill-defined. This section ends at the 800-meter level in a large, very low-angle area below the Triangular Face. A good camp or bivouac could be made here. Climb directly up 45- to 60-degree ice for about 12 pitches to the top of the Triangular Face (2 or 3 pitches of mixed climbing near the top). At this point a heavily corniced and extremely steep-sided ridge leads 150 meters horizontally back from the top of the Face to the base of the ice cliff that bars access to the summit snow slopes. This is the crux of the climb and involves several intricate pitches of weaving in and out among the cornices and sometimes traversing the very hard and steep (80-degree) ice on one side of the ridge or the other. A shovel is useful in removing some of the smaller cornices. From this point the first ascent party discovered a moderate ramp leading through the ice cliff, above which there is 600 meters of snow-slogging to the base of the final summit pyramid. The summit is climbed via a prominent ridge on its southwest side (the route here corresponds with the West Ridge climb).

Descent: To descend, follow the West Ridge route down into the Kahiltna Glacier and then walk the 3 or 4 miles around to the landing site on the Southeast Fork. The trickiest route finding on this descent occurs after you have come down from the summit pyramid and must cross the broad plateau at about 14,000 feet to the point where it meets the West Ridge. This is a narrow spot with huge ice cliffs on either side, and it is hard to locate in a white-out. Therefore, it might be worth taking bearings from a map at the summit and jotting these down (along with distances) in a notebook before descending. At any rate, once you have gotten onto the ridge, you should follow the main spine all the long way down into the Kahiltna. This main ridge runs almost due west, and care should be taken not to accidently follow one of the subridges in another direction. This descent is extremely long (4 horizontal miles) and requires considerable moderate down-climbing and care in dealing with cornices.

Keystone Green Steps

Comments: Total accessibility combined with excellent quality make the Green Steps a very desirable climb. No avalanche hazard as far as can be determined. Frozen waterfall.

Grade: IV-V, WI5.

Season: November-April.

Location: Keystone Canyon along the Richardson Highway about 15 miles north of Valdez. On the east side of the road 2 main falls are visible—the Green Steps is the one on the right (the one on the left is Bridalveil Falls).

Approach: Simply park your car and walk across (or ski) the ice of the Lowe River to the base of the falls. Five minutes.

Route Description: The first pitch is long (35 meters) and takes the left side of the falls to a belay at a low-angle area (WI5). The second pitch diagonals up and right to a belay partway up the next steep section (WI4). The third pitch takes a long, steep pillar to a huge "halfway" ledge (WI5). There is a good bivouac cave at the back of this ledge behind the curtain of ice. The fourth pitch goes up the left edge of the ice once again for 25 meters to a belay ledge (WI5). The fifth pitch is short (20 meters) and leads to a low-angle area at the base of the final 30-meter wall (WI4). The final wall is climbed directly to the top (WI5).

Descent: Two long rappels from trees down the south margin of the ice take you to the halfway ledge. Walk north along the ledge and down into a gully. Down-climb or rappel the gully. Alternatively, 3 rappels from the halfway ledge can be made to avoid the down-climbing.

CANADIAN ROCKIES

Because of the accessibility of many of the climbs, the Rockies are the most important ice climbing area in North America,

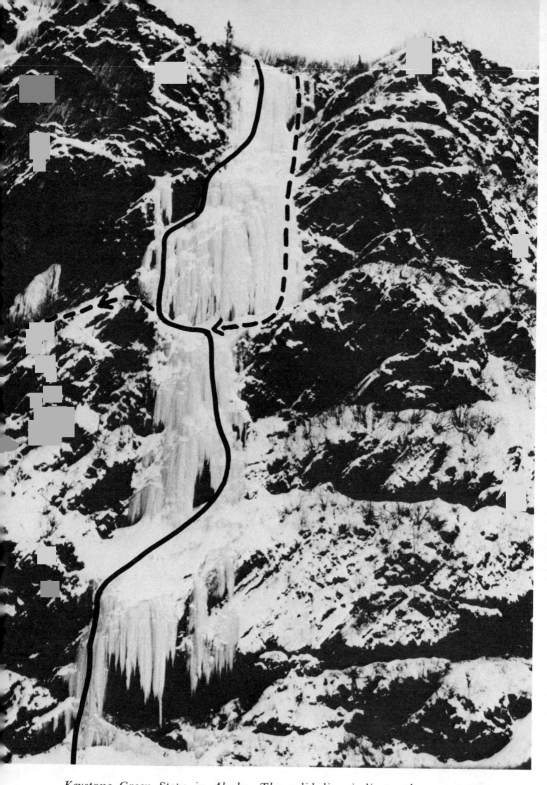

Keystone Green Steps in Alaska. The solid line indicates the ascent route; dotted line, the descent route. (Photo by Jeff Lowe)

This climber is on the last pitch of the Keystone Green Steps. (Photo by Christie Northrop)

even though they are second to Alaska in the quantity and scale of the Alpine ice. And as far as frozen waterfalls are concerned, the Rockies have the biggest and best as well as the most plentiful supply.

As always, where there is good ice there is at least a moderate quantity of inclement weather. In the summer this usually means rain up to about 7,000 or 9,000 feet and snow above. Thus, waterproof outer clothing and bivouac sacks are essential even though windproofs alone might be adequate at the higher elevations. In winter, conditions can be extreme, with 4-foot powder snowfalls overnight and temperatures of 50 degrees F below zero.

Many climbs require an approach of a day or more back-packing, sometimes through absolutely wild, trailless country, where you are more likely to meet a grizzly bear than other climbers. These approaches are an integral part of climbing in the Canadian Rockies, and those who return year after year do so as much for this wilderness flavor as for the climbing.

The most heavily climbed areas in the Rockies lie within the boundaries of Banff, Yoho, and Jasper National Parks, and Mount Robson Provincial Park. The park authorities request that climbers register with them at the outset of their climb and upon return. To ease the pain of this procedure, they have provided self-registration boxes along many of the main highways. If you are unable to locate a self-registration box, it is possible to contact the nearest warden in person or by phone. Tpese procedures seem reasonable since the Park Service does provide a very good rescue service, and if they are aware of your plans, there is less likelihood of a rescue squad being deployed unnecessarily, as might be the case if they were to find an auto full of climbing gear parked at some trail-head for a suspiciously long time.

Beginning in the far northern end of the range, the first mountains that have received much climbing attention are the peaks in the immediate vicinity of Mount Robson (highest in the range at just under 13,000 feet) and Mount Robson itself. Robson, Whitehorn, and Resplendent are the peaks that offer the most extensive ice climbing. Up until now, little winter ice has been climbed in the area despite the obvious possibilities (in the Valley of a Thousand Falls, for instance).

Perhaps the single most concentrated area for ice climbing in the Canadian Rockies is the Columbia Icefield region. This huge mass of permanent snow and ice is ringed by many great peaks in the 11,000- to 12,000-foot range. The climbs vary in length from 300 meters to more than 1,000 meters and in difficulty from easy snow slogs to state-of-the-art classics. Many of the peaks are quite accessible from the road, but others, such as Mount Bryce and Mount Columbia, require a day or so on the approach. There is much winter ice near the Columbia Icefields, particularly near the "big bend" in the Icefields Highway below Athabasca Pass and continuing south to the junction with the David Thompson Highway.

Much ice climbing activity also has taken place in and around the vicinity of Lake Louise. The Valley of the Ten Peaks contains many fine couloir and gully climbs up to 1,000 meters in length as well as the unique bulges of ice found on the North Face of Mount Fay. Ice faces and gully climbs of great quality also are found on Mounts Victoria, Lefroy, Narao, and Popes Peak. In the winter the area has yielded some fine frozen waterfall climbs at the foot of the high peaks.

South of Lake Louise the summer ice routes are scattered over a large area, although many excellent climbs can be found (on Stanley and Assiniboine, for example). In winter, however, the situation is different, with high concentrations of waterfall climbing to be found in the areas of Field, B.C., and Banff. Also, just north of the border in Waterton Lakes International Peace Park there is a high concentration of good winter climbs, many of which have yet to be done.

Mention should be made here (for lack of a better place) of the Interior Ranges of British Columbia. These ranges lie to the west of the Rockies and are separated from them by the Columbia River valley. Better known for their rock climbing (Bugaboos, Adamants, etc.), they contain considerable ice climbing potential, though this potential has been less

The Weeping Wall, one of Canada's many fine winter ice climbs. (Photo by John Roskelley)

exploited than in the neighboring ranges to the east. The most available area is on the peaks surrounding Roger's Pass, which is traversed by the Trans-Canada Highway. Here one can find glacier routes, ice faces, and couloirs up to about 700 meters high.

Two guidebooks attempt to cover the entire main chain of the Canadian Rockies (North and South editions of *A Climber's Guide to the Rocky Mountains of Canada*, available from the American Alpine Club)—a nearly impossible task as the scope is huge enough to fill three times as many volumes. However, the short and often inadequate route descriptions in the guides at least serve to keep the adventure high and keep you on your toes—but not necessarily on front-points! The guides *are* helpful, though, in giving an idea of what had been done up to about 1973 (publication deadline). Unfortunately, many of the finest routes have been completed since that time. For these routes the best references are to be found in the pages of the *Canadian Alpine Journal* and *Mountain* magazine.

So many fine ice climbs have been made in the Canadian Rockies that there is simply too little space to list them all here. However, the climbs below include representative routes of all the kinds to be found. Among the list are gully and couloir climbs, ice faces, glacier routes, "mixed" climbs, and all configurations of frozen waterfalls. This list contains some of the best ice climbs in North America; none are second-rate. It will at least give the reader an idea of where to start and what to work up to. The climbs are loosely organized from north to south.

Mt. Robson, North Face, 700 m, IV, AI3-5
Mt. Robson, Kain Face, 700 m, III, AI3
Mt. Whitehorn, North Face, 450 m, III, AI4
Mt. Kitchener, Ramp Route, 1,200 m, V, AI4, 5.7
Mt. Kitchener, Grand Central Couloir, 1,200 m, V-VI, AI5, 5.9
Mt. Bryce, North Face, 1,700 m (upper ½ ice), IV, AI3-4, 5.5
Mt. Hooker, North Face, 500 m, III, AI3
Mt. Shackelton, North Face, 400 m, III, AI3

Mt. Andromeda, West Shoulder Direct, 500 m, III-IV, AI4
Mt. Andromeda, Photo Finish, 400 m, III, AI4
Mt. Andromeda, Shooting Gallery (North Ridge Couloir), 400 m, III, AI3+-4
Mt. Athabasca, North Face, 400 m, III, AI3
Mt. Athabasca, East Face, 500 m, III, AI3, 5.6
Weeping Wall, 175 m, III, WI5
Polar Circus, 600 m, VI, WI5+
Mt. Forbes, Northwest Face, 500 m, III, AI3
Mt. Patterson, Bluebird Glacier, 800 m, IV, AI3-4
Narao Peak, Northeast Gullies (2), 300 m, III, AI3
Pope's Peak, North Face, 600 m, IV, AI3-4
Wenkchemna Ice Tongue, 500 m, III, AI3-4
Deltaform Couloir, 1,000 m, V, AI4-5
Deltaform Glacier, 700 m, IV, AI3-4
Mt. Fay, Center Bulge, North Face, 250 m, III, AI5+
Mt. Fay, East Bulge, North Face, 250 m, III, AI4
Louise Fall, 120 m, III, WI5
Takkakkaw Falls, 250 m, V, WI5
Tumbling Glacier Couloir, 450 m, III, AI3
Pilsner Pilar, IV, WI5+
Carlsburg Column, IV, WI5r
Mt. Stanley, Northeast Face, 600 m, III, AI3-4
Nemesis, 175 m, V, WI6
Beaurgeau Righthand, 200 m, IV, WI5
Beaurgeau Lefthand, 175 m, IV, WI5+
Mt. Assiniboine, North Face, 700 m, III-IV, AI4

TWO CANADIAN ROCKIES ICE CLIMBS

Grand Central Couloir, Mount Kitchener

Grade: 1,200 m, V-VI, AI5, 5.9.

Comments: A big, objectively hazardous Alpine climb that can be safely done by waiting for cold weather or climbing at night to avoid rockfall. The upper gully contains some very difficult and serious climbing. Bivouac sites extremely scarce.

Season: July-October.

The Grand Central Couloir on Mount Kitchener in the Canadian Rockies. (Photo by Jeff Lowe)

Location: Three miles west of the highway and a few miles north of Athabasca Pass. Mount Kitchener is one of the peaks that border the Columbia Icefields. The Northeast Face of the mountain (with the Central Couloir quite obvious) can be seen perfectly from a turnout in the road about a third of the way down from the top of the steep grade descending from the pass.

Approach: Sign out for your climb at the information center at Athabasca Pass, and then drive 3 miles north to a point at the end of a long, flat stretch of highway. Park your car here. It is at this point that the road ascends a short distance before commencing the final long and steep descent from the pass. Hike down to the river to the west of the road and cross it via a log that spans the narrow gorge into which the water

Two hundred meters from the top of the Grand Central Couloir. (Photo by Jeff Lowe)

funnels at the end of the flat stretch. After crossing the river, follow along the south edge of the trees and ascend west up and over the ridge in front of you (this ridge hides the face of Kitchener from view until you have topped it). Then contour along barren scree slopes into the basin below the face. The head of this basin is attained by traversing the dying glacier at its base. About 3 hours should be sufficient to reach the face from the highway.

Route Description: Climb easy snow (some ice at times) up slopes to the right of the hanging glacier in the bottom of the wall, and then cross over left onto the glacier. At this point you have two alternatives: 1) Go directly up the center of the glacier, crossing the huge crevasse that bisects it below the upper bergschrund, and then cross the bergschrund on the left by way of a very steep pitch; or 2) if the huge crevasse is impassable, cross over to the left side of the glacier, negotiate the 'schrund there, and diagonal up and right to the point where the 2 variations meet at the base of the couloir proper. From this point, about 500 meters of 50-degree ice steepening to 60 degrees will bring you to the narrow upper couloir (AI3-4). The final section begins with a hard, probably mixed pitch in the back of the couloir, which at this point is almost a dihedral. This pitch is the crux of the climb and is poorly protected (AI5). The belay is semi-hanging from pitons in the left wall. One-half of the next lead is also mixed, and then steep ice (65 degrees) leads to a rather broad section of ice below the upper rocky section of the couloir. Two pitches up and right on ice of slightly lesser angle lead to a narrow, chimney-like gully that, in turn, is followed for a pitch up and right to a notch in the rib that borders the main couloir. Short rock steps (the first, 5.9) interspersed with snow and ice slopes lead up the crest of the couloir for 2 pitches to a belay at the base of the summit icecap. One easy ice pitch and one very difficult pitch through the summit cornice bring you to the broad summit.

Descent: Walk southeast about 1/3 to 1/2 mile to where the East Ridge meets the summit icecap. Immediately, you are faced with a deep gash. One rappel (20 meters) deposits you into the gash, and a short but loose bit of rock climbing (4th class) brings you out the other side. From here, a long, relatively gentle snow or ice slope is followed down the ridge crest to the saddle between Kitchener and the small peak known as K2. Contour down and left on snow and scree, heading toward a glacial tarn below the North Face of K2. A moderately steep slope through a cliff-band must be negotiated just above the lake. Wander down to the ridge-top, which you crossed on your approach to the face, and then on down the way you came. Sign in at the information center.

Polar Circus

Grade: 600 m, VI, WI5.

Comments: This is the only YDS grade VI frozen waterfall yet done. It was first climbed using siege tactics, but the second ascent (which was accomplished as the first ascent party was on its way down) was made in a continuous 4-day push. The large basin above gives reason to fear a potential giant avalanche. This is in addition to the normal hazard of small climber-generated slides in the lower-angled and snow-covered portions of the climb.

Route Description: The following is from the *Canadian Alpine Journal,* 1976. Bugs McKeith, a member of the first ascent party, is the author.

This the the huge gully directly above the Cirrus Mountain Campground on the Banff/Jasper Highway, sometimes incorrectly referred to as the Cirrus Mountain Gully. The climbing starts from the valley floor only a quarter of a mile from the road. The initial 6 pitches are comparatively straightforward and include longer sections of 50, 60, and 70-degree ice, with a few short 80- and 90-degree steps, but this whole section can be avoided by walking up the hillside to the left of the gully and traversing in below the first main rock band.

Polar Circus in the Canadian Rockies. (Photo by Jeff Lowe)

A snow basin curves up to the right to the first major pitch, a 150-foot icefall, mainly 70 degrees with a vertical section in the upper half. The next snow basin contains 2 possible bivouac sites: a small rock cave halfway up on the right and a cave formed by a curtain of ice hanging from the lip of a sloping rock roof on the right at the base of the second main pitch, 120 feet, 70 degrees. A narrow snow gully leads up to the "Pencil," the most impressive single ice feature on the route, a 150-foot-long, 6-foot-diameter, totally free-hanging icicle precariously suspended above a multiple mushrooming ice pedestal. Fortunately, the icicle can be avoided, but the 100-foot pitch up the right side of the pedestal is in a potentially dangerous situation. This rears up to a short, vertical section in the first 30 feet then eases back to 70 degrees.

This is followed by a long, easy, but dangerous section across several steep snow bowls which are prone to avalanche. From the top of the pedestal pitch, traverse out to the right for about 200 feet, then straight up past some small trees till it is possible to traverse back left for several hundred feet into the main snow basin at the foot of the final icefall. Set in the base of the main rock face about halfway along the traverse, there is a narrow, 30-foot deep cave with a trickle of running water. With a little work, this could accommodate two comfortably; however, by far the best bivouac is the 50-foot deep cave, 150 feet up to the right of the base of the final icefall. This has a dry, sloping, rock floor in which 2 platforms have been leveled, with plenty room for 4 or more.

Between two 1,000-foot vertical rock walls about 200 feet apart, the final 750-foot icefall rises in 3 tiers. The first tier of 250 feet averages 70 to 80 degrees, with a few short vertical sections and a hanging bolt belay 150 feet up on the right. Above a sloping ledge, the 200-foot second tier starts with a narrow, 50-foot vertical pillar, drops back to 70 degrees, to another hanging bolt belay on the left, then rears up to the vertical for 20 feet before easing again to 70 degrees. The ledge below the 300-foot third tier is flat and about 50 feet wide. On the right side, 4 vertical pillars, separated by short, easier sections and a small belay ledge at half height, lead to the last 100 feet of 70-degree ice, which was running with water. Fifty feet back in a narrow, snow-filled canyon a short, easy ice slope opens out into the huge avalanche basin below the upper southwest face of Peak 10,460 feet, and a short walk up to the left emerges on a previously uncairned top (about 8,000 feet overlooking the gully and the Banff/Jasper Highway.

Descent: Either by the same route or on foot or skis toward the trees and the road to the northwest.

THE NORTHEAST

The Northeast was the site of the earliest exploration by climbers into the harsh winter ice climbs of North America. The now-classic Pinnacle Gully in Huntington Ravine on Mount Washington, New Hampshire, was climbed in the late 1920s by climbers looking for a place to practice ice climbing without traveling to the Alps. Here, there is no permanent ice, but there is plenty of cold and snow in the winter and numerous short to medium-long (300 meter) cliffs over which the melted snow can run and be re-frozen in gullies, chimneys, and on open faces.

Despite the relatively low altitude of the mountains, the winter weather in the northeast can be as harsh as that found anywhere in North America, including Alaska! However, on the lower cliffs and crags such extremes of wind, temperature, and snowfall are not found, and a more relaxed approach can be taken. The climbing can be as easy or as severe as you like, in purely technical terms, but the number of climbs that are both long and severe is somewhat limited. Perhaps the size of the climbs is second to many other areas, but the quality could not be better.

North of the border, in the Canadian province of Quebec, the adventurous climber will find great possibilities for new routes of a length comparable to some of the longer winter routes in the Canadian Rockies. Although most of the ice here remains virgin, the local French-Canadian population has not been idle, and several grade III and IV routes have been made at Baie Eternite and the Malbaie Valley, where a grade V route also has been made.

Further south the main area of mountain ice is the previously mentioned Huntington Ravine, with a wide variety of gully climbs from which to choose. Cannon Mountain offers a small choice of technically difficult routes of four to six pitches, including the popular Black Dike. The routes here have a serious side to them and have seen more than their share of epics—don't think there are no avalanches in New England or long distances to be covered! Cathedral Ledge near

North Conway, New Hampshire, offers a larger variety of one-
to six-pitch climbs in a less remote and friendlier atmosphere
than either Cannon or Huntington Ravine. These climbs
include everything from low-angled verglass over rock to
vertical ice walls. As well as the main areas of New Hampshire, there are many smaller areas such as Frankenstein Cliff
and Crawford Notch that provide the gamut of winter ice
problems.

The surrounding states also have their share of ice. In fact,
good ice climbs can be found as far south as Mount Gonah in
South Carolina. So much for the artificial boundaries implicit
in the words "Northeast ice." Routes such as "Star Shine" on
Mount Whitesides and "Xanadu" on Mount Gonah stub-
bornly refuse to abide by preconceived notions and persist in
providing local climbers with excellent practice.

The *Canadian Alpine Journal* will provide some information for those willing to investigate Quebec ice possibilities.
But the information generally available is scant, and the
climber must be dedicated to ferret out the best areas. The
local climbers undoubtedly have long lists of new routes
hidden from general scrutiny. The climbing in New England
is well covered, however, by a nice little guide called *Shades of
Blue* by Wilcox and Cole. This book, without attempting to
make the ascent for you, gives a good general feeling for the
character of the individual areas as well as enough information to get you to and from your chosen climb. The guide is
available in climbing shops in the East, or you may get it
from Eastern Mountain Sports, North Conway, New Hampshire.

Once again, the list of climbs that follows does not pretend
to include all of the best routes in the Northeast. But among
these climbs you will find examples of the best climbing to be
found in the respective areas as well as *most* of the real
testpieces.

Quebec:
Les Jumelles (Baie Eternite), length unknown, III, WI4
Le Triolet, (Malbaie Valley), 250 m, IV, WI5
L'Equerre (Malbaie), 300 m, V, WI5+

New Hampshire:
Huntington Ravine:
Odell's Gully, II, WI2
Pinnacle Gully, 250 m, II, WI3
Damnation Gully, 300 m, II, WI3

Cathedral Ledge:
Remission, 150 m, IV, WI5+
Repentance, 150 m, III, WI5
Standard Route, 150 m, II, WI5
Thin Air, 150 m, III, WI5

Frankenstein Cliff:
Dracula, 60 m, II, WI5
Drop Line, 60 m, II, WI5-5+
Widow's Walk, 40 m, I-II, WI5+

Cannon Cliff:
Black Dike, 175 m, III, WI5

TWO NORTHEAST CLIMBS

Black Dike, Cannon Mountain

Grade: 175 m, III-IV, WI5.

Comments: The Black Dike was one of the first major solo ice climbs made in America. More than just a "winterized" crag climb, it has a moderately long approach, complete with real avalanche hazard when wind slab is present. There are serious run-outs for the leader on the climb itself and the fairly long descent also might have some avalanche potential. All of these things, when combined with a winter storm, add up to a fine adventure for anyone, no matter how accomplished he or she is.

Location: In Franconia Notch, New Hampshire, the Black Dike is at the back of the obvious cleft in the left side of Cannon Cliff when viewed from the road.

Approach: It is recommended in *Shades of Blue* that you not park your car at the Boise Rock parking area as it is usually not plowed in winter and cars have been towed.

The Black Dike on Cannon Mountain in New Hampshire. (Photo by Peter Breu)

Bryan Becker leading the crux third pitch of the Black Dike. (Photo courtesy of Bryan Becker)

Repentence, Cathedral Ledge. The first ascent was made under these well-iced conditions. (Photo courtesy of Bryan Becker)

The hard lead of Repentence in lean ice conditions. (Photo courtesy of Bryan Becker)

Instead, drive a couple of hundred yeards farther north, and park on the other side of the road. Snowshoes or skis might be useful if the trail through the timber to the talus slope is not broken. At any rate, on the final slope into the bottom of the cleft be on the alert for slab development in the snow-pack.

Route Description: The first pitch goes about 35 meters up the introductory bulges at the very back of the gully (WI2). Another 30-meter pitch, steeper but still not hard, leads to a point where a leftward traverse is necessary to reach the bottom of the Dike proper, which is characterized by a long, very narrow ribbon of ice. The third pitch, which is mixed and hard (WI5), goes left into the ribbon past a fin of rock and then ascends thin ice until the rope runs out at about the same time a sort of alcove is reached. Rock pegs can be found in the dihedral on the right. The next pitch ascends the bulge above on the left and wanders up through moderate bulges. The fifth and final lead is long, somewhat awkward, and ends at trees at the top of the climb.

Descent: Contour off the end of the cliff and struggle through deep snow back to the highway. An alternative that might be better in some cases is to rappel the route when enough ice exists for cutting bollards.

Repentance, Cathedral Ledge

Grade: 140 m, III, WI5

Comments: A generally acknowledged classic of the New England ice scene. The type of climbing will vary with conditions from pure ice to mixed climbing, which consists of jamming between ice and rock. A summer 5.9 rock climb.

Location: The central groove of 3 chimney systems on the northern part of Cathedral Ledge, which is near North Conway, New Hampshire. The climb to the left is Remission and that on the right, Cathedral Direct.

Approach: "The normal summer tourist road is still the best approach in winter with one slight exception, due to the fact that the road is not plowed past the second turn-off into the chalet development. Therefore, head for the northwest corner of the development, where there is ample room for a number of cars."* From here, walk back through the woods to the unplowed road and walk along the road until a final approach can be made to the start of the ice.

Route Description: Three long or 4 regular pitches. It's hard to get lost on this climb. The first and last pitches seem to be the hardest. In lean ice conditions the chimneying between the rock and ice might prove to be the crux.

Descent: Walk north along the top of the cliff and descend to the road via the trail.

THE MOUNTAIN STATES

The mountain states (Montana, Idaho, Utah, Wyoming, and Colorado) have much to offer the ice climber. Wyoming has quite a bit of Alpine gully ice in the Big Horns, Tetons, and Wind Rivers, and Idaho, Montana, and Colorado have small amounts of Alpine ice as well. All of those states have a few small glaciers, and it is possible to find a crevasse to fall into if you try hard. One important characteristic of most Alpine ice found in the mountain states is its relative remoteness. The ice is there all right, but you'll have to walk for it.

Summer weather, when compared with Alaska or the Canadian Rockies, is generally good, but in most ranges afternoon thundershowers are common. The winter ice climber, on the other hand, must be ready for large snowfalls, lots of avalanche hazard, and very low temperatures. In fact, knowledge of avalanche factors is more important to the winter climber though the entire chain of the Rocky Mountains than good ice climbing technique.

The low temperatures that are common in many winter ice climbing areas tend to produce very brittle ice that fractures in large chunks as you climb. So it is imperative that the belayer be positioned out of the fall line at each and every belay.

---

*Wilcox and Cole, *Shades of Blue.*

There is more ice *to be* climbed than *has been* climbed as of this writing.

The only two ranges to which there are decent guidebooks available are the Tetons and Rocky Mountain National Park. *A Climber's Guide to the Teton Range* by Leigh Ortenburger is available from the American Alpine Club, unless it is out of print, and *A Climber's Guide to the Rocky Mountain National Park* by Walter Fricke, Jr., is available in many Colorado climbing shops. There are other guides of a general nature to some of the ranges, but these are of little use to the technical climber other than for reference and to get an overall feel for a particular area. The magazine *Climbing* is published in Colorado and is a good source of information on the latest routes in the intermountain area. However, many of the climbers in Montana do not publicize their routes, so information on that state is scarce. The same anti-publicity phenomenon is evident to a lesser extent in all of the states except Colorado. Once again, the AAJ is a good source for information, usually on major climbs.

A state-by-state survey follows:

Montana: In keeping with the spirit of the local climbers, a list of individual climbs will not be included. However, for those who wish to look for themselves, there is good Alpine gully ice in the Bear Tooth Range and a little in all of the other high ranges of the state as well. In winter there are frozen waterfalls of all shapes and sizes in Glacier National Park. The most climbed winter areas are Hyalite Canyon, 15 miles south of Bozeman, which offers dozens of small to moderately long climbs, and Pine Creek Valley, containing a couple of classic routes of about 60 meters as well as much more. Other good places are Mystic Lake and the mountainside south of Nye, both of which are in the Beartooths.

Idaho: Little information is available regarding ice climbing in Idaho. Several winter snow gullies have been done in the Sawtooths and on Devil's Bedstead near Sun Valley. Undoubtedly, there is winter ice around also. There is at least one good waterfall that drops into the Snake River Canyon near Twin Falls.

Wyoming: Wyoming has the greatest amount of Alpine ice of all the mountain states in the Big Horn, Teton, and Wind River ranges. Of the climbs in these ranges, only those in the Tetons and, to a lesser extent, the Wind Rivers are generally known in spite of the fact that a lot of ice climbing has been done.

An Alpine ice gully on the North Face of Sulphur Peak in the Wind River Range, Wyoming. (Photo by Mike Kennedy)

Some of the best Teton ice routes are:

Black Ice Couloir, 700 m, IV, AI3, 5.6
Enclosure Ice Couloir, 400 m, III, AI3, 5.6
Northwest Couloir, Middle Teton, 300 m, II, AI3
Middle Teton Glacier, 600 m, III, AI2-3
Run-Don't-Walk Couloir, Mt. Owen, 500 m, IV, WI4
Thor Peak Couloir, 400 m, III, AI3
Prospector Falls, Death Canyon, 100 m, II, WI4
Sentinel Gully, Death Canyon, 100 m, II, WI4

Some good Wind River ice routes are:

North Face, Mt. Jackson, 300 m, III, AI3
Tower 1 Ice Gully, Mt. Helen, 400 m, III, AI3, 5.5
Tower 2 Gully, Mt. Helen, 300 m, III, AI2-3
Warrior Gully, Cirque of the Towers, 500 m, II, AI2
Northeast Couloir, Arrowhead Peak, III, AI3

Utah: For all intents and purposes, there is no Alpine ice in Utah. In winter the situation changes, and there is very good water ice around Ogden, Salt Lake City, and Provo. Following is a list of some of the better climbs in the respective areas.

Ogden:
Mahlen's Peak Waterfall, 100 m, II-III, WI5-5+
Ogden Canyon Falls, II, 75 m, II, WI5
Great Amphitheater Gully, 200 m, III, WI4
Northeast Face, Original Route, Mt. Ogden, 300 m, III WI4

Salt Lake City:
Great White Icicle, Little Cottonwood Canyon, 175 m, II, WI3

Provo:
Stewart Falls, 150 m, III, WI5-5+
The Fang, 120 m, II-III, WI4-5
Miller's Thriller, 150 m, II, WI4

Finger of Fate, 150 m, II-III, WI5
Stairway to Heaven, 250 m, III, WI5

Colorado: The high mountains of Colorado have a few nice surprises in store for those who are willing to look around for permanent or semi-permanent Alpine ice. And in winter the whole mountainous part of the state has numerous waterfall and gully climbs. Some of the most important climbs, in the most concentrated areas, are listed here.

Rocky Mountain National Park:
Taylor Glacier, 350 m, II, AI2
Taylor-Powell Couloir, 400 m, III, AI3
Powell Chimney, 350 m, III, AI3
McHenry's Notch Couloir, 400 m, II-III, AI2-3
Notch Couloir, Long's Peak, 500 m, III, AI3
Flying Buttress Couloir, 500 m, III, AI2-3

Vail:
Rigid Designator, 40 m, I-II, WI5

Glenwood Canyon:
Left Pillar, Glenwood Icefall, 150 m, II-III, WI5
Center Route, Glenwood Icefall, 150 m, II, WI4
Right-Hand, Glenwood Icefall, 150 m, III, WI5
Hidden Falls, 120 m, II-III, WI5

Telluride:
Ames Fall, 150 m, IV, WI5+
Bridalveil Falls, 120 m, IV, WI5+-6

Ouray:
The Skylight, 90 m, II, WI4-5
Cascade Falls and Gully, 175 m, III, WI4-5
Little Bear, 100 m, II, WI4
Kennedy's Gully, 200 m, II, WI4-5
Gravity's Rainbow, 200 m, III, WI5
North Face, Mt. Sneffels, 300 m, II, AI2

TWO CLIMBS

Black Ice Couloir, Grand Teton

Grade: 700 m, IV, AI3+, 5.6.

Comments: An American classic. This route description deals with the *complete* couloir even though it is quite easy to bypass the lower section by using the West Face route. There is much rockfall caused by tourists on the Owen-Spaulding route, which crosses above the couloir. Take a good late summer climb after the guided traffic on the Grand slows down.

Normal Season: July-September.

Location: Above Valhalla Canyon (which is itself above and east of Cascade Canyon) on the west side of the Grand Teton, tucked in under the North Face of the Encloser.

Approach: Sign out at Jenny Lake Ranger Station. Either take the commercial boat across Jenny Lake or take the trail up the canyon for several miles, past Storm Point on the north. Cross to the south over Cascade Creek on a logjam and climb the hillside above, which leads to Valhalla Canyon. Stay on the west side of the stream that descends from Valhalla Canyon for a short distance, and then cross over to the timbered slope on the east when that seems appropriate. The hike to Valhalla might take 4 hours or so. A bivouac in the canyon is good as it not only allows you to get an early start in the morning but is a lovely place with a little stream cutting through patches of green, boulder-strewn meadow. But please don't camp on the fragile lawn. The Black Ice Couloir leads from the top of the boulder field at the head of Valhalla to the notch between the Enclosure and the main mass of the Grand Teton. Lower down, a couple of low-angle snowfields are separated from the main couloir by a rock band to the left of the base of the huge yellow prow on the North Face of the Enclosure. The main couloir leads up from here through a couple of icefields, then steepens through a right-hand turn for the final stretch to the Upper Saddle.

Opposite page: The 175-meter Ames Fall is one of the finest Colorado ice climbs. (Photo by Mike Kennedy)

Looking across from the West Face of the Grand Teton into the upper section of the Black Ice Couloir. (Photo by Mike Lowe)

Climbing in the middle section of the Black Ice Couloir. (Photo by Mike Lowe)

Route Description: Climb the previously mentioned lower snowfields to the base of the higher of two leftward-slanting ramps. Climb a pitch and a half up the ramp (which at first is a sort of low-angle chimney). The initial pitch usually is mixed ice and rock. At an indented and broken area of the rock wall above, leave the ice and climb up and right about 50 or 60 feet past a short, steep slab in a corner, and belay at the end of a traverse ledge that leads straight right into the bottom of the upper couloir. Once back on the ice, follow it for 10 or 12 pitches to its end. The final 4 or 5 pitches are the steepest, with bulges of 65 degrees. It usually is possible to belay from either ice or rock pitons as you prefer. You can easily reach the top of the Grand from here, also.

Descent: Follow the regular descent trail down gullies and short rock steps south and down from the Upper Saddle (where the climb ends) to the Lower Saddle and then east down the Granite Canyon trail to the Lupine Meadows parking lot, where, hopefully, you will be able to hitch a ride back to your car (if you have one) at Jenny Lake.

Bridalveil Falls

Grade: 130 m, IV, WI5+-6.

Comments: Colorado's finest, hardest, and most consistently well-frozen waterfall. It never gets any sun in winter and is often in condition for climbing when little else is. Avalanche hazard on approach and descent is high during and after storms, but the climb itself is free of snow slides.

Season: Usually late December to early April.

Location: About 1 mile above and southeast of the Idarado Mine, east of Telluride. It is the obvious ribbon of ice hanging off the cliff underneath an old castle-like building (a defunct power station).

Approach: Park your car at the end of the plowed road just east of the mine, out of the way of mining company vehicles. Don your cross-country gear and ski up to the base of the falls, following a summer Jeep road. It's a 30-minute to 1-hour trip.

Opposite page: Bridalveil Falls in Colorado. (Photo by Greg Lowe)

Route Description: Four fairly long pitches meandering through overhangs and bulges, following the line of least resistance. This varies a bit from year to year, but it usually lies directly up the center for 2 leads, then up the right side on the third pitch, and finally up the lower-angle exit chimney. The first 3 leads are all WI5 or harder, and the final pitch is WI4. Good belay stances usually can be found on top of some of the bulges. Very often natural handholds in the ice make progress easier than using tools. Also, much natural protection can be arranged.

Descent: Post-hole through the snow up the bank behind the "castle" for 25 meters or so until you come to a road that leads east along the top of the cliff band. Follow this to the slope, which slants down along the base of the cliff, back to your skis. Take care of this slope if there is any sign at all of instability in the snow-pack (i.e., depth hoar or much freshly fallen snow). Under very unstable conditions it might be better to rappel the down-climb using bollards to save on gear.

CALIFORNIA

Ice climbing in the Golden State either is frustrating or ecstatic. Waiting for a certain waterfall in Yosemite to freeze or a Sierra gully to assume its desired glassy consistency has become an occupation for many climbers. But when the waiting is over and the moment finally arrives, it's worth it because the beauty of climbing in Muir's "range of light" can't be surpassed. Ice climbing in Yosemite? Outrageous!

All this waiting is due to the particular climate of California's mountains. There is not enough sub-zero winter weather to keep the waterfalls frozen, yet there is so much sticky snowfall that the gully climbs in the high mountains generally don't shed their sloppy layer of last winter's snow until September or later. An early fall snowstorm easily can wipe out a whole summer's slow development.

But this is not to say that there is no dependable ice.

A climber on the second pitch of Bridalveil Falls. (Photo by Mike Lowe)

Generally, you can rely on the ice in Lee Vining Canyon or at June Lake during the winter months, and certain Sierra gullies are so steep (Mendel Couloir, for instance) that they seem to hold less snow than others and therefore come into condition sooner and stay good longer. Many of the climbers in the eastern Sierras (centered around Bishop) are against publishing the new climbs that they have made. Thus, only climbs that have been mentioned in print somewhere else will be detailed here.

In the northern part of the state there is some Alpine ice and glacier climbing on Mount Shasta, which is an anomaly of the California scene. In the nearby Trinity Alps there is a small amount of more typical gully ice, but you'll have to hunt for it. Near Lake Tahoe, at Donner Summit, there is occasionally some water ice, and Eyeore's Ecstasy at Lover's Leap has provided at leas one party with an icy winter epic. But the bulk of California ice is to be found from the Palisades on south past Mount Whitney. Included in this area are all of the best gully climbs and, of course, Yosemite, with its lovely waterfalls, a few of which sometimes freeze. Last but not least, Tahquitz and Suicide Rocks, southeast of Los Angeles, occasionally ice up in a way that would do justice to the finest Scottish winter areas.

Following is a short list of some of the more popular and difficult routes.*

Mt. Dana (gully), 300 m, II, WI2
Bloody Mountain (gully), 500 m, III, WI2-3
Ice-Nine (Mt. Mendel), 350 m, IV, WI5
Mendel Couloir, 350 m, III, WI3
U-Notch (North Palisade), 300 m, II, WI2
V-Notch (North Palisade), 300 m, III, WI3

Yosemite:
Cloudburst (Clouds Rest), 175 m, III, WI4
Sentinel Falls, 150 m, II, WI4
Silver Strand, 150 m, III, WI5
Widow's Tears, 300 m, V, WI5
Silver Strand, 150 m, III, WI5
Widow's Tears, 300 m, V, WI5

---

*Credit should be given here for partial use of a list of ice routes in *Ascent,* 1971, by Yvon Chouinard.

TWO CALIFORNIA CLASSICS

Widow's Tears

Grade: 300 m, V, WI5.

Comments: Several years ago I wrote in the *American Alpine Journal* that the Widow's Tears is "America's most beautiful ice climb." Since that time my opinion has not changed. Situated at the back of a huge granite amphitheater that looks out on Ribbon Falls and the West Face and Salathe Wall of El Capitan, the Tears is a silver snake of ice that

Widow's Tears in Yosemite Valley, California. (Photo by Greg Lowe)

beckons the climber with a two-pronged tongue, promising both adventure and satisfaction. This route, unfortunately, is often not in good condition.

Location: Half a mile east of and above the Wawona Tunnel on the road leaving the valley toward Fresno. The shorter climb to the right of the buttress that forms the Tear's right retaining wall is the Silver Strand.

Approach: Park your car at the viewpoint at the east mouth of the tunnel. Walk down the road until you find a likely spot to climb straight up through brush and small trees to the beginning of the climb.

Route Description: Kevin Worral has supplied the following information on the first ascent (there has been no other), which followed the line of least resistance:

> We found 11 pitches of fifth-class climbing and made 2 traverses on snow, one unbelayed and the other fourth class. We bivouacked twice, the first night on the left side of the fall at the top of the first section and the next night on the right side of the fall on the big ledge beneath the final step. We had to stop climbing early in the afternoon each day to hide under overhangs from falling ice.
>
> The climb consists of 3 distinct sections: 4 moderate to easy pitches on the first section, beginning on the right and working up and left to the first ledge (bivvy); then we traversed right on the snow and climbed the right side of the next section in 3 pitches, with the first of these being the crux of the climb on 90-degree ice, and the other 2 slightly easier. We traversed back left on the snow ledge below the final section, which consisted of 4 long pitches. Mark took a long fall onto a tied-off screw on the ninth pitch. He finally used a few screws for aid to get past this extremely rotten and steep piece of ice.
>
> *Descent:* Walk west through deep snow along the rim, past Silver Strand Creek and Inspiration Point (the actual rock feature, not the viewpoint on the road behind the rim) until a long gully can be found that can be followed down to the road. The gully bottom is ice covered with snow and is full of bushes. Expect a struggle.

Mendel Couloir

Grade: 350 m, III, WI3.

Comments: A steep and remote climb. Until the ascent of a thin ribbon of water ice called Ice-Nine, which lies on the rock face to the left of the couloir itself, this was considered the hardest gully in the Sierras. It is still *the* classic.

Location and Approach: See Steve Roper's *A Climber's Guide to the High Sierra.*

Route Description: Cross the bergschrund of the Mendel Glacier and ascend steepening neve toward the right-hand couloir through the upper wall. Follow the couloir to the top,

The Mendel Couloir in the Sierra Nevada, California. (Photo by Ken Cook)

in about 10 pitches, over bulges reaching 65 degrees. Belays can be made from nuts in the rock at the side of the gully.

Descent: A scramble down the northwest ridge leads to a col at the top of a snow couloir. Descend the couloir, and this deposits you back in the glacial basin beneath the North Face of Mount Mendel.

Climbing in the Mendel Couloir. (Photo by Ken Cook)

THE NORTHWEST

Glacier climbing has become almost an independent branch of mountaineering in the Northwest. Thousands have slogged up the normal routes on the glacier-covered volcanoes of Mounts Baker, Hood, St. Helens, and Rainier, people who wouldn't know what to do if they ever found themselves on rock or even real ice.

More experienced technical climbers have discovered that not all glaciers were created equal. Some have interesting crevasse problems; others have steep slopes, jumbled icefalls, or towering seracs on which to play. As well as the volcanoes, the Cascade peaks of Shuksan, Maude, Redoubt, Fury, Forbidden, and on and on, offer snow climbs of all sorts and an occasional pitch of harder Alpine ice.

The relatively warm but stormy winters produce fantastic amounts of rime and snow-ice, which might leave almost no rock exposed. The first winter ascent of the North Peak of Mount Index, for instance, which was made in 1963, required crampons to be worn all the way. In summer it is a pure rock route. The Pacific Northwest, like California, suffers from a lack of consistently low winter temperatures at the low elevations where waterfalls normally are found, and so far not much water ice has been discovered. The 200-meter Drury Falls in Tumwater Canyon is an important exception.

One big problem with much of the climbing is its lack of accessibility. In summer any area without a trail is hidden behind clumps of devil's club, slide alder, and other forms of obnoxious foliage that makes travel miserable. The heavy winter snowfalls ensure, of course, that there will be avalanches in the steep-sided canyons that are the usual avenues of approach to the high, remote peaks, although the hazard is not quite as great as in the Rocky Mountains.

These obstacles have served to keep all but the most accessible of America's Alpine mountains free from the overuse seen in the Tetons, Rocky Mountains, and Sierras. The Northwest mountains are insurance against the time when the more easily abused ranges have lost all of their wilderness qualities.

Fred Beckey's *Climber's Guide to the North Cascades,* in North and South editions, covers most of the best snow and ice climbing to be found in the Northwest. Nicholas Dodge's *Climber's Guide to the Mountains of Oregon* deals with that state.

From north to south, here are some of the better climbs:

North Face, Mt. Redoubt, 700 m, IV, AI3
North Face, Mt. Maude, 600 m, III, AI2
Entiat Icefall, Mt. Maude, 500 m, III, AI3
Northeast Face, Forbidden Peak, 500 m, III, AI2
Nooksack Cirque Icewall, Mt. Shuksau, 350 m, III, AI3
Stewart Glacier Couloir, Mt. Stewart, 500 m, III, AI3
Ice Cliff Glacier, Mt. Stewart, 500 m, III, AI2-3
Snow Creek Wall, Country Club Route, 300 m, WI5
Drury Falls, 200 m, III, WI4

Mt. Rainier:
Nisqually Icefall, length unknown, III, A2-3
South Tahoma Headwall, 1,000 m, III or IV, AI2
Sunset Amphitheater Headwall, 500 m, III, AI2
Sunset Ridge, 1,200 m, III, AI2
Edmunds Headwall, 1,200 m, III or IV, AI2-3
Ptarmigan Ridge, 1,200 m, III, AI2-3
Liberty Wall, 1,200 m, IV, AI3
Liberty Wall Direct, 1,200 m, IV or V, AI3
Liberty Ridge, 1,300 m, III or IV, AI2
Damocles Rib, Willis Wall, 1,200 m, V, AI3 (with direct finish
    through ice cliff)
Central Willis Wall, 1,200 m, IV, AI3
Curtis Ridge, 1,000 m, III, AI2-3

Mt. Adams:
Lyman Glacier, length unknown, III, AI2-3
Wilson Icefall, length unknown, III, AI2-3
Wilson Glacier Headwall, length unknown, III   AI2-3
Victory Ridge, 1,000 m, III or IV, AI2-3
Yokum Ridge, Mt. Hood, 700 m, III, AI3

TWO NORTHWEST CLIMBS

Damocles Rib (Willis Wall), Mount Rainier

Grade: 1,200 m, V, AI3.

Comments: The thick ice cliff near the top of this climb makes it an objectively hazardous route. But for those climbers willing to lessen the time spent under the cliff by moving fast, it is perhaps not overly dangerous. This description includes a direct finish over the summit ice cliff. This finish will vary greatly in difficulty, depending on the condition of the cliff.

Season: May-June (normal).

Location: On the north side of Mount Rainier, the farthest west rib on the Willis Wall, which is bordered by the Liberty Ridge on the right and the Curtis Ridge on the left.

Approach: Sign out at the Carbon River entrance to Mount Rainier National Park. Drive to the end of the road along the

Damocles Rib on Mount Rainier, Washington. (Photo by Larry T. Clark)

Carbon River and park. Take the trail up to the Carbon Glacier, and when it seems reasonable, cross the glacier, which is badly crevassed later in the season, and head for the base of the rib.

Route Description: Follow the line of least resistance. It is possible to stay almost completely on snow and ice, but you might find a rock pitch or two if you stay on the crest of the rib. The bergschrund becomes almost impassable later in the season. At the top of the rib, climb below the ice cliff diagonally to the right until ymu find a lower-angle ramp leading through it in the vicinity where the cliff jogs straight right toward the top of Liberty Ridge. Climb a final snow slope to Liberty Cap (the north peak of Mt. Rainier).

Descent: If you have left gear at the base of the face, you might want to go down Liberty Ridge, which requires care but is not really difficult. Just remember to stay west of the crest if any difficulties present themselves. Any number of other possibilities also are available. See Beckey's guide for these.

Yokum Ridge, Mount Hood (winter)

Grade: 700 m, III, AI3.

Comments: A true winter classic with an "Alaskan" flavor.

Location: On the west side of Mount Hood.

Approach: From Timberline, ski to Illumination Saddle. Then traverse and descend the Reid Glacier to the base of the ridge. Not much more can be said, except climb the ridge, weaving in and out of the towers in whatever manner possible until the ridge broadens and merges with the summit slopes.

Descent: Via the normal route back to Timberline.

One Man's Frostbite

Writing this book has been like doing a difficult new ice climb. Since it had not been done before, a detailed scrutiny of the problem was required (deciding what to write about), after which the gear to be taken had to be carefully sorted (what to omit, what to include). And then the final approach had to be made (the book to this point). But wait, we're not through yet. Chapter 5 is the climb!

FEAR AND CONFIDENCE

It is July 20, 1967. A hot Teton afternoon. Summits hover in the haze above Cascade Canyon, whose pines and stream-crossed meadows provide the background for a 16-year-old's approach to his first ice climb. The boy's boots leave perfect waffle-prints in the dust of the old trail as he takes long strides in order to keep up with his older partner. They are headed toward a logjam in the creek across from the rocky bulk of Storm Point.

The boy's mind is filled with stories of ice climbing in the European Alps: spindrift avalanches on the White Spider, Rebuffat's climb of the North Face of the Matterhorn. Scary stories, they are, yet beautiful. Descriptions of a world he fears but wants to know: cold bivouacs, glistening mornings, snowy days, the crunch of steel points biting into ice. But that dream lives across an ocean in mountains that are fairytale castles to the boy. The hills in his mind are romantic sounding but vague and shapeless when compared to the crags that surround him now. The boy scans the Guide's Wall of Storm Point; he remembers the texture of the rock and the surge of blood and muscle that were required by the twin cracks of the last pitch.

The young man and the boy come to the ford in the stream. They cross the network of naked timber, rucksacks a challenge to their balance, and on the other side they stoop to drink. The cold water echoes in the mouths as they start up the hillside to the hanging canyon of Valhalla. Behind them the sun drops below a craggy ridge, and they climb puffing through the fir trees.

The forest thins, straggles, ends, disgorges the man and the sweating boy. The boy's thighs groan with painful relief at the final steps into twilight Valhalla. The man turns and watches the boy drop his rucksack onto the rich turf that covers a portion of the basin. A gentle gurgle fills the air with sucking and popping from the streamlet that bisects the meadow in a string of half-loops. They make camp against a square boulder. The man brings water in a mess tin; the boy lights the stove.

While the soup is heating and sending beef smells into the air, the man points steeply up at the West Face of the Grand Teton, which looms above them in the dusk. He tells the boy that between the main peak on the left (which is just losing its final Alpine glow) and the lower shoulder silhouetted on the right lies the Black Ice Couloir. The boy tries to see into the gully through the increasing darkness, but his straining eyes can discern no secrets.

Opposite page: " . . . a world he fears but wants to know."
(Photo by Michael Kennedy)

Curled up on his foam pad and bundled in a down parka against the square rock, the man snores. The boy shivers under the stars. His legs are cold. He tries to see himself on the ice of the Couloir, but he has trouble with the vision. He feels young and afraid at the thought of the steep gray ice he has heard about around fires at Climber's Camp. He recalls tales of rockfall caused by tourists on the Owen route, which crosses a rock-strewn ledge above the Couloir. He imagines the strain on calf muscles. They say it is like pitch after pitch of unprotected 5.8 slabs. The boy's fears keep him awake and shaking slightly in waves, synchronized with the rasping breath of the dark figure next to him. He watches Orion creep across the sky and waits wide-eyed for morning.

Years pass, seasons bloom and wilt, freeze and thaw. The boy makes many ice climbs and loses his fear but not his respect. He becomes a young man himself.

The young man is in the Canadian Rockies. He emerges from his tent at the Columbia Icefields campground just as a faint glow begins to wash the stars from the eastern sky. He stretches in the cold air. A month of climbing has left him feeling strong and supple, mentally relaxed, aggressive in an adventurous way. The clear predawn promises a perfect day for climbing, but one partner has gone home and another won't arrive for another two days. He could spend the day photographing the bighorn sheep on the grassy hillside above the campground or perhaps read in the sunshine. But there's a nice new route to do over on the west shoulder of Andromeda. The young man decides he'll take a peek at that, instead. The date is July 21, 1973.

Dressed in wool knickers, tattered green cardigan, and brown balaclava, the young man throws his ice axe and a small pack containing a hunk of cheese, cagoule, and crampons into the front seat of his beat-up old car. Headlights glow like cats' eyes in the fading dark as the vehicle chugs past tents, vans, campers, and a log cook-shelter, bouncing softly down the dirt road to the junction with the highway. He turns west onto the paved road.

During the three-mile drive to the parking lot at the sightseeing concession ("See the wonders of the Athabasca Glacier from the comfort of an enclosed snowmachine) the young man is treated to one of his favorite sights: glaciated mountains awakening to the first light of a new day. On his left are Mounts Athabasca and Andromeda; the Snow Dome and Kitchener are to the right; the tongue of the Athabasca Glacier laps down from the icefield between the two sets of peaks.

At the parking lot (which lies below and between Athabasca and Andromeda) he grabs the blue pack and ice axe from the seat. The door slams as he hops out into a slight breeze. It's chilly, and he wastes little time in shouldering the small load and hopping over the guardrail onto the surface of the moraine. The wooden-shafted axe feels familiar and good in his hand as he scrambles up an unstable hill toward the glacial bench that contours beneath the North Ridge of Andromeda and gives access to the face he wants to climb.

The bare ice of the shelf is weathered like an old man's face and littered with small dark stones that have fallen from the rocky buttress of the ridge. Crunching noises punctuate the young man's footsteps as he rounds the corner of the ridge to see the top of the west shoulder turn pink at the first touch of the sun. A shallow arete of ice interspersed with rocky steps falls 1,800 feet directly from the glowing summit into the small glacier that still separates the young man from the climb. Yes, a good route, he thinks, taking a deep breath. But to get to the base he must first negotiate a jumble of ice blocks the size of houses and then traverse the upper glacier, whose crevasses still remain partially hidden by last winter's snow.

He avoids most of the short icefall with surprising ease by hugging the base of the North Ridge. A lattice-work of ramps and bridges winds around the edge of one serac and spans a gap between two others. But the upper glacier is more worrisome. It's a gently rolling quarter-mile of half-covered crevasses. Easy terrain, but dangerous. It is with more than respect in his heart that he bends forward at the waist and begins the probing and poking with the shaft of his axe that will continue until he reaches the foot of the climb. The young man presents a humble figure bowing his way across the snow, dwarfed by the rock ridge behind him and the ice-wall in front.

Arriving below his planned route, the young man rests a few minutes. The sweat streaking his face from cheeks to temples evaporates as he sits on his pack and straps crampons to boots. The sun has reached a point two-thirds down from the top of the face, but it's still cool where the young man sits. He takes a moment more to eat a piece of cheese and regain his composure. The obvious problems of the route (wide bergschrund, steep ice, snowed-up rock, summit cornice) seem far preferable to the unseen holes of the glacier.

(Photo by Mike Kennedy)

Crossing the bergschrund is difficult. At its narrowest it still yawns six feet wide, with a bottom too dark to see. He breaks the overhanging lower lip back until a platform can be made to support his weight. He makes a quick calculation. If he lets himself fall forward, will he be able to span the gap with the full length of his body plus outstretched arms? He decides he can. The shock of contacting the upper wall is greater than expected. Then, maintaining the bridge with one hand, he swings the axe with the other and plants it well in the ice of the face. Feet swing from the lower edge of the split, and the young man is established on the climb.

For 50 feet the ice is tilted up at 70 degrees. He wishes he had brought along an ice hammer to complement the axe, but the steep part is soon behind him. Conditions are excellent. Hard snow, ice that takes points like cork. As he climbs farther, he enters the sun. He pauses a moment on the 50-degree slope to change to dark glasses and store his sweater in the pack. The rim is etched white against a lake-blue sky. He lopes upward, climbing a narrow gully through one rock band, skirting another by a couloir on the right, and regaining the ice arete again 500 feet from the top. He's feeling as light as the ice crystals that sparkle in the air, immune to the old avalanche runnels that swoops down to the glacier.

Crampons grate on limestone as he climbs through an unavoidable cliff 100 feet below the summit. The top of the rock tapers into snow that gets looser and steeper. Right under the jutting cornice it reaches 80 degrees, and he has to plunge the shaft of the axe and all of one arm into the snow for purchase.

The cornice juts out a full 15 feet directly above him. An insecure leftward traverse of 40 feet brings the young man to a place where the cornice has fallen, and there is only a 7-foot vertical step barring him from the top. But a full half-hour is required to carve a groove through the snow. At last, however, his careful efforts are rewarded, and he flops safely onto the flat summit.

He stands up and brushes the snow from his clothes. A

panorama of his favorite mountains fills his view. Slowly turning full circle, the pyramid of Mount Forbes lies to the south. Double-summited Bryce is to the west, sun gleaming on its ice faces. The broad shield of Athabasca can be seen to the east, and the snow domes of Kitchener, the Twins, and Columbia rise out of the icefield to the north.

Looking down through the notch from which he recently emerged, he sees the dots of his crossing on the small glacier at the bottom of the face. He sees how the small glacier tumbles down into the mile-wide stream of the Athabasca. He watches as a tiny red bug with 30 people inside it winds its way down a bulldozed road from the snowmobile concession on the lateral moraine to the flat surface of the broad ribbon of ice.

The young man gives a single whoop of joy and then begins the descent.

GRABBING FRIENDSHIP BY THE ANKLE

Colorado

Michael Kennedy is a resident of Aspen, Colorado, and editor of *Climbing* magazine. Prior to March, 1977, I had met and talked with Mike only once. However, on that occasion, which occurred in the kitchen of my brother's house in Eldorado Springs, Colorado, I was favorably impressed. Many good climbers are very intense, seemingly about to burst at the seams. That sort of intenseness always has been difficult for me to handle, and I have a tendency to shy away. By his reputation, I knew Mike was a good climber, and when we sat down for a cup of coffee together I was halfway prepared for a tense and awkward situation. Our talk, however, was very enjoyable.

Among other things, we talked about independent attempts that we both had made on the East Face of the Moose's Tooth, a huge Alaskan wall that is yet unclimbed. When I asked him the reason for his party's failure, a smile broke through his beard. "At our high point we were hit by an avalanche of ice

Opposite Page: " . . . a figure high on a frozen waterfall . . . ." (Photo by Jeff Lowe)

blocks," he said. "One of our anchors was ripped out, and one of our packs was smashed where it sat on a ledge. That was enough for us." He concluded, "We go out of there fast; man, we were *freaked*!"

Mike was no arrogant, macho climber but a man who admits being scared and can smile at his own fear. As we continued to talk, sip coffee, and size each other up (yes, I'm certain Mike was taking *my* measure as well), I sensed a fairly strong feeling that the lanky fellow across the table from me would be a good partner in the high mountains. When Mike got up to leave and shake hands, I said, "Let's get together and do a climb sometime." "For sure," Mike agreed. "I'd like that a lot."

When in March, 1977, I found myself in need of another instructor for an International Alpine School ice-climbing course, I thought of Mike. We wouldn't exactly be climbing together, but it would be a good chance to get to know each other and gauge the value of that first impression. By the end of the course, when we were having a rather boisterous end-of-course celebration at the Outlaw Bar in Ouray, I knew I had been right about Mike.

After a long winter of teaching, I had run out of energy and inspiration. Mike had sensed this and doubled his own output: setting up most of the top-ropes on the icefall, demonstrating techniques in an enthusiastic (and competent) way, taking groups of students on two consecutive days up long and difficult climbs, and giving them the experience they had come for. Having done all that, he accepted my thanks for a job well done, saying simply, "That's what I'm being paid for, isn't it?" and then buying me a Heineken.

I asked him over the beer if he would be interested in going to Alaska in June to try a couple of new routes on Mount Hunter and Foraker. My cousin George Lowe and I had been planning these climbs all winter but needed a third partner. "Would I?" he answered. "Is the Pope Catholic?"

Alaska

We met in the airport in Anchorage. George had come from California—Mike and I from Colorado. George and Mike had never met. It was a blind date and we were all very aware of that fact. Nervous. George and Mike were all good humor and politeness: "Ho, ho," George said when he greeted us at the baggage claim, "glad to see you guys made it. You must be Mike." They shook hands like two businessmen.

I found myself nodding in an inane but hopeful way. Yes, nod, that is Mike, and, nod, yes, that fellow with the young face and hearty greeting is George, the physicist-climber with whom you'll soon be climbing. I was the matchmaker and I prayed that George's serious mien and Mike's casualness would complement each other rather than clash, as can happen so easily on hard climbs.

Two days later we were lying in George's North Face Morning Glory tent at the base of the North Face of Mount Hunter. We had taken the train from Anchorage to Talkeetna and then were flown by pilot Jim Sharp to our present location in the heart of the Alaska Range, near Mount McKinley on the Southeast Fork of the Kahiltna Glacier.

The first objective of the trip could be seen through the arched opening of the tent door. The Northwest Spur of Mount Hunter rises more than 7,000 feet from the Southeast Fork to the summit at 14,573 feet. If we were successful on Hunter, we planned to try a new route on the 10,000-foot-high South Face of 17,400-foot Mount Foraker, which is on the other side of the Kahiltna from our basecamp.

But first we had to climb the spur that swept up in front of us. As Mike exclaimed when we first landed on the glacier, "That's a training climb?" Our Alpine-style plans seemed a bit flimsy when compared to the obvious strength of the mountain's defenses. It didn't help to know that three good-sized expeditions already had failed on the same route.

But we already had made our preparations: cached spare skis at the base of the West Ridge, which was to be our descent route, and loaded our packs with bivouac gear and food for five days. We planned to climb during the Alaskan night, which in June never becomes darker than twilight farther south. That way we hoped to avoid the sloppy snow conditions that were certain to exist during the day. The reggae sounds of Bob Marley and the Wailers helped Mike and me endure the waiting, but George glanced up from his book occasionally with a half-hidden look of disst on his face that seemed to say, "What are we, rock groupies or climbers?"

At ten-thirty Jimmy Cliff was singing, "The harder they come . . . the harder they fall. . . . " George punched the stop button. The sun was off the face; our wait was over. Outside the tent not much was said as we donned our skis and roped up for the short approach to the base of the spur. The silence was almost as heavy as our packs as we began to ski up the nearly flat glacier. We were spaced 150 feet apart on 2 ropes, and above the noise of the skis as they slid over the crisp surface, conversation was not easy to maintain. None of us really wanted to talk anyway. It was enough just to be starting a big climb, the snow-covered peaks all around us huge and impressive in the subdued light.

An easy snow-bridge over the bergschrund put us on the climb. At the base of the route we traded skis for crampons. We climbed simultaneously most of the way up the lower spur. Mushy snow covered the ice to start. We made a quick front-point around the end of a rock band, threatened by a drooping serac. Hard-breathing effort took us up steep, unstable snow. The crest of the spur dropped away on both sides and curved up to taper into an ice bulge that barred the way. But the bluish-white ice looked good. A core of ice extruded from a screw as it went in. There was the click of a carabiner. Basecamp looked small already, 1,500 feet below, and the wings of the orange tent seemed like a tiny butterfly lost in a sea of snow and crevasses.

George's crampon points loomed above us as Mike and I belayed him up the steep ice bulge. Mike moved fast up a corridor of snow between ice towers where the crest became broader. We huffed to keep up, taking short rests leaning on our ice axe. The white outline of the slope above us became sharply etched against a sky of opaque blue as the sun rose from its shallow dip below the horizon. The ridge was broken by a flat at the top of the lower section, below a pointed ice face we had dubbed "The Triangle." It was 6:00 A.M. We rested and had a bite of cheese and zucchini bread. Weighty food, perhaps, but more sustaining than "freeze-dried." We had done more than one-third of the climb.

It was nice to sit on the packs and eat and gaze around at the waves of peaks lapping at the sky. I looked over at McKinley, which rises above a row of intervening mountains, and wondered if there were people over there at this very moment staring back, taking a break from the effect of climbing that massive hill. But my reverie soon was brought to a halt. "We've made good time up to here," said George, "but the real climbing is just beginning." My vision followed the sweep of his hand up the 1,500-foot ice-wall and came to rest at the sharp summit. I knew George was right.

The ice face itself looked straightforward enough (though with our heavy packs, we had to belay), but something we couldn't see from where we sat had us all a bit worried. From the apex of "The Triangle" there is a narrow, corniced ridge leading horizontally back from the summit of our spur, connecting it with the main mass of the mountain. From the airplane on the way in it had looked like a ripsaw blade, points coated with marshmallow syrup sticking up vertically. "Let's get started, then," said Mike, who already was standing up and re-shouldering his pack.

On the face, the leader trailed both ropes and anchored them to two ice screws when they ran out. The other two climbed simultaneously, one being belayed by the leader and the other belaying himself with a Gibb's Ascendeur. The climbing alternated between good snow and hard ice. The angle varied from about 45 degrees to perhaps 60 as we headed for the right-hand containing ridge, which looked as if it would offer easy going for the last few hundred feet to the top of the face. At belay stances we chortled at our good luck with the weather and joked about making the summit in a few hours. Mike led the last pitch to the ridge up a steep and insecure trough.

Our "easy" ridge turned out to be a nightmare of insecurity. George struggled up through mushrooms and cornices made of snow that had the consistency of porridge but not the cohesiveness. It was rotting in the sun, drooping everywhere, threatening to fall into the space around us, perhaps taking us with it as well. George took hours on his lead, attempting to compact the snow so that it would hold his weight. It was like trying to swim up a knife-edge of sand, tilted at 60 degrees. Finally, George yelled down that he had a belay. "But don't fall, I don't think it'll hold." Mike and I shot worried looks at each other as I started to follow.

Several pitches and much time, sweat, and worry later, the three of us were ensconced on a small ledge we had shoveled out of the snow just under the very top of the face. Almost comically our rope was draped around the nearest mushroom. We were not very much cheered by by the "security" this provided, but it was all that was available. Mist and light snow moved in. We had climbed for 19 hours to get to this place. The horizontal ridge that led back from the present location was only 500 feet long, and after that it looked like walking to the summit. But those 500 feet were the worst bit of climbing terrain any of us had ever seen.

We brewed soup on our little ledge and tried to talk ourselves into believing the situation was not quite so glum as it appeared to be. But I had a terrible feeling in my stomach, as if at any moment the whole mountain would fall. "It's impossible," I said, and believed. There was no strong opposition to that viewpoint, but we agreed to rest where we were until the early morning hours had solidified the snow as much as possible; then we would give it a try. After all, we were only 500 feet from success, yet more than 4,000 feet above basecamp. We tried to sleep.

At one o'clock in the morning I started out on the traverse of the ridge. Somehow I had hogged the lead. The suspense of waiting behind seemed worse than whatever difficulties the ridge could offer. I used the shovel in place of my axe because a great deal of snow would have to be removed to get to something that would support body weight. I quickly lost myself in the task, shoveling like a wildman trying to tunnel back to sanity.

" . . . thoughts of success began to enter my mind . . . ." (Photo by Mike Weis)

The cornices overhung the narrow and incredibly steep ridge on both sides. The trick was to make a trail through them without making them fall. Things went well at first, and after a short while, the rope between Mike and I stretched tight. He began to follow since there was no place to establish a belay. I began to enjoy the tunneling and crawling and balancing, and thoughts of success begin to enter my mind as

I approached the halfway point along the ridge. I was happy, too, in a way, as I started to carve on a particularly nasty lump of snow.

With a sickening "WHOOMP," it suddenly felt as though the earth had begun to rush inward on itself. But that implosion was only in my head. The cornice had fallen and me with it. I did not feel too much fear (will Mike and George hold me, or will they go, too?), but I did a lot of flailing about with my feet in a futile attempt to stop tumbling. All in a flash, I felt my left crampon points snag the ice. My ankle made a snapping sound, and I felt tendons rip! Then, just as suddenly, my fall stopped. I was dangling on the rope, sixty feet below the side of the ridge. George was yelling to see if I was all right. "Yeah," I replied, "but I think my ankle's broken."

After a prolonged struggle to regain the ridge, during which the only assistance Mike or George could offer was a tight rope, I crawled back along the path I had so recently chiseled and greeted Mike at the place where he was straddling the ridge. It was the only such place around—and he had landed there after being jerked off his feet by the force of the fall! The clouds had descended around us, and it began to snow again. "Well," Mike said, "I guess we get to go down now, huh?"

The descent of the ice face took a long time. First George would rappel down and set up an anchor from an ice screw or rock piton in the bands that crossed the face. Then it would be my turn to hop one-legged down to George. Next, Mike would slide down. The whole process was repeated numerous times, and as the storm got heavier, spindrift began to flow down the face in a continuous sheet. Strangely, our humor was good. We told each other jokes at the stances. George and Mike accused me of creating an excuse to get back to see a lady I had met in Talkeetna.

While we were doing the next to last rappel before reaching the flat area below the face, I stood alone with George at the anchor. "You know," he said, "I'm glad Mike was along on this one. He's solid as hell." Then Mike came down and George slid off on the next rappel. I chuckled to myself to hear Mike say, "Man, it's great to be with a guy like George in a situation like this. Hey, what're you laughing about? You finally flipped out on us, or what?"

Opposite page: The corniced ridge on Mount Hunter. (Photo by Mike Kennedy)

We bivouacked again on the flat at the base of the face. George and Mike also made a perfect splint for my ankle from several rolls of adhesive tape and the aluminum staves of my pack. Another day was consumed in getting off the climb, but we finally arrived at our skis, which stuck out of the snow like outstretched arms. Relaxing before the final leg of the journey back to basecamp, I lounged back on an ensolite pad, and the mountain loomed above the injured ankle I was holding up in the air. "That was kind of fun." I said to no one in particular. Maybe it was just the euphoric effect of the Percodan that I finally had allowed myself to take, now that the dangerous part of the descent was over.

Epilogue

The same day we finished the retreat from the Northwest Spur, I was flown directly to Anchorage. Doug Geeting, another pilot from Talkeetna, just happened to land on the Southeast Fork to drop off another party of climbers shortly after we arrived at camp. At Providence Hospital in Anchorage it was discovered that I had suffered a severe sprain and two bone chips.

Mike and George returned to Hunter and completed the route a few days later. After that, they went around to the south side of Foraker and made a ten-day ascent of the "Infinite Spur." These achievements were made even more satisfying to the climbers by the new bonds of friendship that had formed between them. Mike was later to write:

"I felt completely comfortable climbing with George. There were no ego games between us, no competition, and the experiences of the last . . . days had brought us very close."

MIND MARATHON

Let us live for the beauty of our own reality.

The Chink*

*From the novel *Even Cowgirls Get the Blues* by Tom Robbins.

Toward the end of one winter, Bill Johnson, a staff writer for *Sports Illustrated*, rang me up long distance.

"Would you be willing to do some ice climbing for an article we have in mind," he asked. An image of a solitary figure high on a frozen waterfall popped into my head.

"Sure," I said, "if I can choose the climb."

"No problem there," replied Bill. So we made arrangements to meet at the end of March in the little ski-resort town of Telluride, Colorado. Bridalveil Falls is situated above the Idarado Mine at the head of the mountain valley a few miles east of town.

Telluride: the appointed day arrived. Bill and his daughter Tina and Willis Wood, a photographer on assignment for the story, and I sat down to breakfast at the Iron Ladle. Outside the front window the town was snowless under a summer-hot sun. Young women, brown as cherrywood and clad in halter tops, walked the Old-West streets or lounged on the wooden benches that grace the store fronts.

Bill peeked over the piece of cheese omelet he had cut and speared with his fork. The omelet waggled in front of his neatly trimmed beard as he phrased the question that was on all of our minds.

"Hell, Jeff, is the ice going to be safe to climb today?"

"I think so," I lied, "but we won't know for sure until we ski into the base. That is, if there's any snow left to ski on up there."

Scratching under his English-style cap, Willis said, "Well, we've got good light anyway."

Bridalveil could be seen from the parking lot at the mine, where there was a three-foot snow-pack that was shrinking almost visibly. Speculations were voiced as to whether the ice that we could see still standing was any good. I held my tongue, certain it was not, though the shaded nook in the cliffs where the falls are situated insured that Bridalveil would remain in condition longer than any other climb in the state. Besides, after all the fuss, I felt obligated to go through the motions.

Bill tossed a bottle of red wine into his pack along with several oranges and candy bars. "For lunch and a toast to success," he said. Still no comment. Removing all unnecessary clothing, we began the ski to the base of the icefall. There would be no climbing today, I thought silently. The approach up the scenic valley was thus rendered carefree. I had a couple of hours in which to relax.

But by the time we arrived in the boulder- and snow-filled catch basin beneath the ice, there had been a change in the tone of the afternoon. We discovered that it was *cold* there in the shade. Even the act of packing a platform on which to stand once we had removed our skis was not sufficient to warm our bodies. Sweaters and parkas appeared from packs and were gratefully donned. Furthermore, there was no sound of running water. Though the ice was thin under some of the bulges and the dark underlying rock showed through, it was *not* melting.

While the others stood around to "ooh" and "ah" at the ice, I made preparations to climb, explaining, "I'll probably just climb a pitch or so—up to that thin spot beneath the overhang—then rappel down." So besides strapping crampons to boots and removing the ice axe and a North Wall hammer from my pack, my pre-climb activities included uncoiling a rope to trail behind me, not for safety, as it would simply dangle from my waist, but for use on the rappel. Also a few ice screws were included to use in anchoring the rappel. In spite of all these precautions, there was even now a little voice in the back of my head whispering, "It will go." But for the moment I was successful in suppressing that sound.

As I began to climb, my mind was in neutral. No hopes. No expectations. Just an exploratory attitude to see what the ice was like. The rope that dangled from my waist was my umbilical to earth. "As soon as the ice gets bad," I thought, "or the climbing too difficult for comfort, all that is necessary is to place an ice screw and rappel off the fall." In a way, the security that this knowledge provided was comforting but comfort and concentration don't mix very well. To climb unprotected on Bridalveil, and do it safely, would require *total* concentration. The rope began to tug at the back of my mind, asking, in a way, for the attention I could ill afford to give it.

The first 60 feet are known as "The Apron" and the ice inclines at an angle of about 75 degrees. Huge cauliflower-like formations characterize this section. The climbing is relatively easy. It's a simple matter of maintaining balance over the crampons while working up through the slots and bulges, using ice clumps for handholds, and occasionally planting the pick of the axe. Working the body into position this way is a pleasure. There was a further delight: here, at least, the ice was good. Firm as a solid old oak and only slightly brittle.

Too quickly, "The Apron" lay below, and the ice reared up vertically for 50 feet, capped by the first *crux* of the climb, a 3-foot overhang. Was that gentle downward pull on the rope real or imagined? No matter. Mind Control said, "go up; the ice is good."

In the steep section below the overhang are two pillars, spaced about two feet apart. The ice in the shallow trough between them was thin enough in places to make visible the green moss growing on the rock beneath. By stemming between pillars, one foot on either side of the trough, balance could be maintained, weight kept over the feet to save the arms for when they might really be needed. I placed the picks of my hand-tools at the back of the trouv primarily as a precaution against falling over backward. The rope trailed down, its final coils still among the feet of my small audience, who, I supposed, were watching intently although they were of my hand-tools at the back of the trough primarily as a regardless of how many people observed it.

A long time was required to find a way past the overhang. The problem was bold but the solution intricate. I lost myself in an effort to find the combination that would unlock the passage. The underside of the ledge was a cathedral apse. At the apex it was necessary to scrunch up as high as possible and perform an ablution: with the ice hammer dangling from

its wrist loop in my right hand (left hand hanging onto the axe where it had been placed diagonally around the edge of the roof), I reached into a slippery hole at a point where the ice began to jut out to form the ceiling. A small indentation was found that was just enough, but my fingers were being washed in waves of cold that seeped through their wool covering. They soon would be numb and useless. "Stay calm," mind instructed body. Vision became acute, and time slowed until there was plenty.

A crampon-shod left boot came floating into view, headed for a purchase on a boulder-sized bump at the lip of the overhang. Contact was made and points bit into the ice, small flakes fracturing off and drifting down out of sight. Then the right foot flowed from underneath the edge and came to rest near the other. The right hand left its hold and regrasped the ice hammer. The silver blade arced through the air, and a piece of ice above the overhang burst slowly as the hammer thunked solidly. My body straightened once again into a position of balance, and time resumed its normal pace. Beads of perspiration dripped from my forehead onto my glasses. The mind relaxed, but only slightly.

A few moves higher there was a good ledge for standing. The rope at my waist gaveu hard jerk at the same moment I stepped onto the ledge. This time there was no question. The rope was stuck somewhere below, tangled in icicles. As if inanimately refusing to go on, all attempts to free it from above proved futile. It seemed the penance of the overhang would grant me no heaven. Feeling quite defeated, I placed two ice screws as an anchor, attached the rope, and rappeled to the source of the problem, which, once there, was easily remedied by a simple flick. Cleared, the rope swooped earthward invitingly tempting me to follow it.

My body wasn't tired, but my mind wanted to rest. In spite of that desire, the little voice that earlier had whispered of an unlikely possibility, now was heard a bit larger, and it had worked its way into the realm of conscious consideration. As I reclimbed the section that had been descended, well-protected

Opposite page: " . . . maintaining balance over the crampons while working up through the slots and bulges . . . ." (Photo by Greg Lowe)

by the rope from above, the decision to continue was reached. But there were still some nagging doubts about the remainder of the route: what about the rotten-looking section at halfway? Was there a way around the huge overhang at 300 feet? More urgent doubts crowded in regarding the length of time that such intense concentration could be maintained without a lapse. I would continue the climb, yes, but I hadn't the conviction yet to leave the rope.

The second 100 feet of climbing contained no unusual problems, and a controlled but enjoyable rhythm began to direct my moves. The ice that had appeared from below to be rotten was not; there was just a subtle change in hue, perhaps due to the millions of tiny air bubbles trapped within. "The climb *will* go," the inner voice shouted. And softer, but with conviction, "Get rid of the rope; it's only distracting you." I was happy with these commands but couldn't bear to watch the rope—and my attachment to it—fall away summarily. I left it tethered to an ice screw and continued.

Unleashed from the rope, both body and mind felt much lighter. No thoughts of failure. The entire entity became aligned with gravity, but only as a reference point for balance. Real difficulties seemed to disappear under the energy of a unified approach. Body obeyed mind and liked it, almost *understanding* its purpose. In turn, mind appreciated the way body fed it stimuli. Smooth, cold, blue, monochrome. A brittle clatter. Swing, breathe. Connect, connection. Almost— almost—almost—. . . .

Unexpectedly, there was a change in orientation as if the ice were falling forward in front of me. I realized after a moment that my vertigo was the result of a reduction in the angle of the ice. Adrenaline spurted through my system when I looked up to see that an easy slope was all that separated me from the top of the climb. But the adrenaline had to be overruled. To rush the climb now would be folly. To climb all that way with concentration and then wander off on the last bit would negate the whole event. Every step—to the end—must be made as carefully as every other.

"Body obeyed mind and liked it . . . ." (Photo by Mike Gilbert)

The deep, water-worn gorge at the top of the falls was the exit tunnel from the immediate experience of the climb to the conceptualized world to which I now returned. Relief came in jerks and spasms. First, a welling of tears; then a restraining. Next, a more enjoyable satisfaction and relaxation of control. Once again the world formed itself for familiar, joyful examination. Crags and sky, wispy cirrus clouds, pine trees and snow, wool, steel, flat, forest.

The whistle down at the mine blew, indicating a change of shift or closing time. The sound echoed through the hills. The sun began to set down-valley above the Lilliputian town of Telluride, and I began the slog through knee-deep snow that would take me around the edge of the cliff that harbors Bridalveil and down to the newly remembered people at the base of the falls.

A beer and companionship would suit my fancy just now.

AFTERWORDS

Ice climbing is a path of approach to a world apart. It is a simpler, more dynamic world than the one we are used to. Death is close. Social concerns drop away as so many inconsistencies in a logical argument. The truth of an individual's nature begins to emerge as instinct shows its old forgotten face.

There is a certain purity in engaging in what some would call a "useless activity." When the ice climber confronts the overhang, he does so with the knowledge that no material gain will result from the completion of his task. Yet he commits his whole physical/mental/spiritual being to climbing the bulge. He is confident that when he is done, the satisfaction will outweigh the effort.

However, the person with gravity tugging at his heels also senses the absurdity of the situation. In the face of great difficulty the climber's mind might revolt against the apparent stupidity of the challenge. But on second thought, he sees that no greater inherent meaning infuses that other life he has left

" . . . a ceiling of a hundred icicles . . . ." (Photo by Mike Kennedy)

behind, except the meaning with which he chooses to invest it. And so, as Don Juan says, he simply must "choose the path with heart."

This morning two people sat with their dreams in a cold room. Several candles illuminated the interior of the abandoned building that had sheltered them last night. No affinity for the flickering candlelight was evident in the geometric corners of the room, and the darkness of the corners somehow was oppressive to the climbers. They wasted no time in packing their gear for an escape from the room, which for them had acquired all the ambience of a tomb.

Later, they climbed up to a hole in the ice with a ceiling of a hundred icicles and a floor of frozen motion. In some superficial aspects the cave resembled the room in which they had passed the night: it had an entrance, a floor, and a ceiling—all enclosing a space that could be occupied by people.

But the climbers felt the essential difference of this natural cave from its manmade counterpart. The light showing through the translucent walls lent a sense of magnificence to the emotions of the pair. And whereas they had felt entombed in the confines of the building, discovering the cave was like finding a bright new home.

When they again found themselves out on the exposed face, there were no questions in their minds, and they were not looking for answers. They were, purely and simply, climbing.

"They were, purely and simply, climbing." (Photo by Lance Wilcox)

Index

A

ABCs of Avalanche Safety, The, 45
Aiding on ice, 101
Alaska Mountaineering and Hiking, 126
Alaskan climbs
  Keystone Green Steps, 131, *illus.* 132, 133
  Mount Hunter, Northwest Spur, 129-31, *illus.* 128, 129
Alpine hammers, 62
Alpine ice, xii, 82, *illus.* xii
Alpine mountaineering, history of, 3-22
American Alpine Journal, 126
Ames Fall, Colorado, *illus.* 159

Ascending and descending moderate ice, 84, *illus.* 86
Ascending extremely steep snow slopes, 76-77, *illus.* 77
Avalanches, 44-47, *illus.* 46
Axe swinging technique, 91-92

B

Bacon, Paul, 17-18
Baker, Ken, 19
Balmat, Jacques, 3
Basic clothing, 152
Becker, Bryan, *illus.* 149
Beckey, Fred, 11-12, 19, 23, 44
Bell, Charlie, 14-16, 38
Bertulis, Alex, 15, 38

Bivouacing on ice, 55, *illus.* 55-56

Bivouacs and snow caves, 79-80, *illus.* 79

Black Dike, Cannon Mountain, 147-52, *illus.* 148, 149

Black Ice Couloir, Grand Teton, 159-62, *illus.* 38, 160, 161

Boles, Glen, 19

Bollards, 110-11, *illus.* 111

Bouchard, John, 27, *illus.* 27

Bragg, John, 28

Bridalveil Falls, Colorado, 28, 162-64, *illus.* 29, 50, 163, 165

Brittle Two-step, 80, *illus.* 80

Brown, Rob, 25

C

California climbing routes, 164-70

　Mendel Couloir, Sierra Nevada, 169-70, *illus.* 169, 170

　Widow's Tears, Yosemite Valley, 167-68, *illus.* 167

Callis, Pat, 16, 23

Canadian Rockies climbs, 131-44, *illus.* 136

　Grand Central Couloir, Mount Kitchener, 138-42, *illus.* 139, 140

　Polar Circus, 142-44, *illus.* 143

Carman, Pete, 34-35

Cauliflower ice, 104, *illus.* 105

Chapman, Mark, 31-33, *illus.* 32

Chouinard, Yvon, 18-19, 23, 34-35

Climbing, 126

Climbing guides, 120

Climbing in North America, 2

Climbing in a snowstorm, 49, *illus.* 48

Coale, Frank, 17-18

Cornices, 47

Craig, Bob, 12

Crampon bindings, 58

Crampons, 56-58

Crampons, use of in ice, 83-84, *illus.* 84

Crampons, use of in snow, 78, *illus.* 78

Crevasses, 47-48, *illus.* 47

D

Damocles Rib, Mount Rainier, 173-74, *illus.* 173

Dark glasses, 55

Davis, Dan, 16

Deadmen, 65

Deadmen, use of in snow belays, 111-12

Denali. *See* Mount McKinley

Descending low-angle ice, 84-85, *illus.* 85

Differences between rock and ice climbing, x-xii, *illus.* x, xi

Double ropes, use of, 108

Douglas, David, 3

E

Eberl, Dennis, 34-35

Ellena, Nick, 19

Elzinga, Jim, 39

Evans, John, 17-18

F

Face masks, 54-55

Faint, John, 19

Falling climber, 51
Falling ice and rock, 49-50
Farrand, Joe, 19
Footwear, 53-54
Foster, W. W., 5-7
Front-pointing with the axe in
    the piolet ancre position,
    illus. 91

G

Gear, general care of, 62-63
Glissading in snow, 75-76
Gordon, Don, 12
Gowan, Dakers, 41
Grading systems for ice and
    rock, 121-24
Grand Central Couloir, Mount
    Kitchener, 138-42, *illus.* 139,
    140
Grassman, Eckhard, 19, 23, 36,
    39
Greenwood, Brian, 19, 28

H

Hand- and foot-tools,
    sharpening of, 62
Hanging belay, setting up of,
    116-17, *illus.* 116
Harrer, Heinrich, 11-12
Haston, Dougal, 41
Heckmair, Anderl, xiii, 10
Headlamps, 55
Helmets, 54
History of Alpine
    mountaineering, 3-22
Homer, George, 28
Hummingbird hammers, 62

Hummingbird Ridge, Mount
    Logan, 16-18, *illus.* 16, 17
Huntington Ravine, 8-9

I

Ice axe belaying methods, 109-10
Ice axes, 58-61, *illus.* 59
Ice axes, carrying correctly, 72,
    illus. 71
Ice-climbing hazards
    Avalanches, 44-47, *illus.* 46
    Cornices, 47
    Crevasses, 47-48, *illus.* 47
    Falling climber, 51
    Falling ice and rock, 49-50
    Weather, 48-49
Ice-climbing routes
    Alaska Range, 126-27
    Mountain states, 153
    Northeast, 145-53
Ice-climbing technique
    Aiding on ice, 101
    Ascending and descending
        moderate ice, 85, *illus.* 86
    Ascending low-angle ice, 84,
        illus. 84
    Belaying with an ice axe, 109-
        10
    Descending low-angle ice, 84-
        85, *illus.* 85
    Encountering special
        problems, 101-8
    Front-pointing on steep ice, 95
    Moving simultaneously on
        Alpine ascents, 117-19
    Practicing on steep ice, 95-97
    Protecting thin ice, 117
    Route-finding on ice, 83
    Setting up a hanging belay,
        116-17, *illus.* 116

Stemming, 100, *illus.* 100
Step-cutting on ice, 82-83
Testing the ice, 90-91
Using bollards, 110-11, *illus.*
    111
Using the brittle two-step, 80,
    illus. 80
Using crampons, 83-84, *illus.*
    84
Using deadmen in snow
    belays, 111-12
Using double ropes, 108
Using ice hammer, ice axe,
    and crampons, 86-90, *illus.*
    87-90
Using the monkey hang, 97-
    100, *illus.* 98, 99
Using natural handholds, 104,
    illus. 102
Using natural formations, 112
Ice hammer, ice axe, and
    crampons, use of, 90
Ice pitons, 63-64
Ice screws, 63

J

Jaquot, Ray, 15
Johnson, Bill, 193
Jones, Chris, 2, 19, 35, 36, 38
Jones, Jim, 36

K

Kahl, Heins, 19
Kain, Conrad, 4-7
Kain Face, Mount Robson, *illus.*
    4
Kallen, Urs, 19, 23
Kanzler, Jim, 23

Kennedy, Mike, 41, 183-91
Keystone Green Steps, 131, *illus.*
    132, 133
Kinds of ice
    Alpine ice, 82
    Neve, 81
    Water ice, 82
Kor, Layton, 18-19

L

LaChappele, Edward, 45
LaFleur, A. J., 28
Locke, Charlie, 19
Long, Dick, 17-18
Low temperatures, 51
Lowe, Dave, 39
Lowe, George, 38, 41, 184-91,
    illus. 25
Lowe, Greg, 23-26, 28, *illus.* 24,
    26, 38, 40
Lowe, Jeff, 29-31, 36, 38-89, 184-
    91, *illus.* 21, 31, 102, 118
Lowe, Mike, 40

M

MacCarthy, A. H., 5-7
MacCarthy, Jim, 13, 19
MacKay, Lloyd, 19
Macquarie, Chas, 41
Mahlen's Peak, 23
Mahre, Dave, 12, 14
Mendel Couloir, Sierra Nevada,
    169-70, *illus.* 169, 170
Meybohm, Henry, 11-12
Miller, Steve, 14
Mixed ice and rock, 105-7, *illus.*
    106, 107, 118

Monkey hang, 97-100, *illus.* 98, 99
Mount Athabasea, *illus.* 20
Mount Deborah, 11-12
Mount Hunter, corniced ridge of, *illus.* 191
Mount Kitchener, north face, *illus.* 36
Mount McKinley, south side, *illus.* 41
Mount Robson, 9-11, *illus.* 6
Mount Robson, north side, *illus.* 5
Mountain, 126
Mountain states climbing routes Ames Fall, Colorado, *illus.* 159
   Black Ice Couloir, Grand Teton, 159-62, *illus.* 160, 161
   Bridalveil Falls, Colorado, 162-64, *illus.* 163, 165
   Teton routes, 156-62, *illus.* 160, 161
   Wind River Range, Wyoming, *illus.* 155
Mountaineering: The Freedom of the Hills, 48, 66
Moving simultaneously on Alpine ascents, 117-19

N

Natural handholds, use of in ice climbing, 104, *illus.* 102
Natural formations, use of for belays or protection, 112
Nelson, Anton, 13
Neve, 81
New England Ice Grades, 122
North Wall hammers, 62

Northeast climbing routes, 145-53
   Black Dike, Cannon Mountain, 147-52, *illus.* 148, 149
   Repentence Cathedral Ledge, 152-53, *illus.* 150, 151
Northwest climbing routes, 171-74
   Damocles Rib, Mount Rainier, 173-74, *illus.* 173
   Yokum Ridge, Mount Hood, 174

O

O'Brien, Lincoln, 8-9
O'Dell, Noel, 8-9
Okonek, Brian, 12
Ortenburger, Leigh, 69
Outram, James, 5

P

Paccard, Dr. Michel, 3
Parkas, 53
Patey, Tom, 51
Pickets, 65
Pinnacle Gully, 8-9
Placing ice screws on pitons, 112-14, *illus.* 113
Placing snow pickets, 112
Plunge step in snow-climbing, 75
Polar Circus, 142-44, *illus.* 143
Porter, Charlie, 41
Pound-ins, 64
Practicing on steep ice, 95-97
Prater, Gene, 14
Protecting thin ice, 117

R

Raeburn, Harold, 22
Repentence Cathedral Ledge,
     152-53, *illus.* 150, 151
Robinson, Doug, 51
Rock and ice-climbing,
     differences between, x-xii,
     illus. x, xi
Rotten ice, 104
Route-finding on ice, 83
Route-finding on snow, 73
Run-Don't-Walk Couloir, 40,
     illus. 40
Rupley, John, 19

S

Salathe, John, 13
Scott, Chick, 19
Scott, Doug, 41
Scottish grading system for ice,
     121-24
Screw-placing tools, 64-65
Scully, Frank, 18
Self-arrest in snow-climbing, 70-
     73
Setting up a normal belay with
     ice screws, 114-16, *illus.* 115
Sharpening hand- and foot-tools,
     62
Sleeping bags, 53
Slings or wrist loops, use of, 93-
     94, *illus.* 93
Snow-climbing, 69, *illus.* 70
Snow-climbing technique
     Ascending extremely steep
         slopes, 76-77, *illus.* 77
     Cutting steps in snow, 76

Distributing your weight, 69
Finding the route in snow, 73
Glissading, 75-76
Using crampons, 78, *illus.* 78
Using the plunge step, 75
Using self-arrest, 70-73
Using step-kicking, 74, *illus.*
     74
Snow-covered rock, 108
Snow shovels, 65
Steck, Al, 17-18
Stemming, 100, *illus.* 100
Step-cutting on ice, 82-83
Step-cutting on snow, 76
Step-kicking in snow, 74, *illus.*
     74
Stevens, Hazard, 3
Summer, Bill, 41
Summit, 126
Swedlund, Herb, 15

T

Terrondactyl hammer. *See* North
     Wall hammer
Testing the ice, 90-91
Teton climbing routes, 156, *illus.*
     160, 161
Thin ice, 103-4, *illus.* 103
Thompson, Gray, 35, 36, *illus.*
     37
Tube screws, 63-64

U-V

Underhill, Robert, 8-9
Vockeroth, Don, 19
Von Trump, Philemon, 3
Vorg, Ludwig, xiii, 10

W

Washburn, Bradford, 126
Water ice, xii-xiii, 82
Waterproof ropes, 109
Weather, 48-49
Widow's Tears, Yosemite Valley,
    31-33, 167-68, *illus.* 167
Weis, Mike, 28-31, 38, *illus.* 30,
    31, 106
Wickwire, Jim, 15, 38
Wilcox, Rick, 28
Willis Wall, Mount Rainier, 14
Wilson, Jim, 17-18

Wind River Range, North Face
    at Sulphur Peak, *illus.* 155
Wood, Rob, 28
Worral, Kevin, 31-33
Wright, Dave, *illus.* 34

Y-Z

Yokum Ridge, Mount Hood, 174
Yosemite Decimal System for
    grading rock, 121-24
Zero hammer. *See* North Wall
    hammer